Child *of*
Our Time

A Young Girl's Flight
from the Holocaust

R U T H   D A V I D

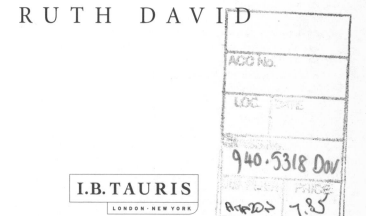

I.B. TAURIS
LONDON · NEW YORK

Published in 2003 by I.B.Tauris & Co Ltd
6 Salem Road, London W2 4BU
175 Fifth Avenue, New York NY 10010
www.ibtauris.com

In the United States and Canada distributed by Palgrave Macmillan,
a division of St. Martin's Press
175 Fifth Avenue, New York NY 10010

ISBN 1 86064 789 8

A full CIP record for this book is available from the British Library

Typeset in Minion by Dexter Haven Associates, London
Printed and bound in Great Britain by MPG Books, Bodmin

In memory of those who died.

In gratitude for the survivors.

For Margaret and Simon Finch

You have asked me for the story of my childhood and I promised to write it as honestly as I could. It is the truth as I remember it from yesterday and perceive it today. You will notice that I have pegged my story to the relevant historical facts of the time, well known to all, except those who for doubtful reasons of their own deny the truths of history. Because mine was not a normal childhood, I never wished to burden you with my sadness as you were growing up. Therefore I told you little. Because you are thoughtful and sensitive, you did not persist in questioning me. Perhaps we were at fault in this suppression. I now feel I should have spoken more; this would have helped me to come to terms with feelings of hatred and resentment. It might have been good for you and others to hear from me how my life was. My childhood was not unusual for my time in history; what was unusual was my good fortune. One-and-a-half million children like me are not able to indulge in their memoirs today.

I was not gassed, burnt, shot or used for medical experiments. Nor did I have to suffocate under the weight of the dead in a massacre or a mass grave. I had contemporaries, schoolmates and friends whose lives were expendable in the sight of the representatives of the master race. Through the human goodness and the vision of some and with the practical help of others, my life was saved. As a child I found it difficult to be grateful for this. I yearned to be with my family, wherever they were, whatever their danger. I did not want to be in a distant land among strangers. As I grew up, I recognized my good fortune but wondered, why me? Why was I saved when so many were not? I do not know the answer. I am grateful that I have been able to live and to know you. I would like to thank you and all my friends and Friends (the Quakers) for help, support, encouragement and love.

Contents

Pictures

1   Moritz Oppenheimer, my father, was a factory owner and respected employer in the Odenwald.

2   Margarete ('Grete') Oppenheimer, my mother, was a university-educated woman, a mathematician raised in a cultured environment.

3   Mina Dümig, our devout Catholic housekeeper, was an extraordinarily loyal pillar of support. She was like a second mother to me.

4   The idyllic view of pre-war Fränkisch-Crumbach, as seen on this postcard, masked the social and political turbulence experienced by the village.

5   Our family house, built in 1907 by my father. My father and his first wife Klara are at the window. He was forced to sell it in 1938.

6   Me, aged nine. Last photo in Germany.

7   The Oppenheimer children in 1938 before Werner's departure (clockwise: Werner, Hannah, Ernst, Ruth, Feo and Michael). Our last photo together.

8   With my best friend Elfi (left) in Tynemouth, 1940.

9   My sister Hannah (left) and brother Ernest when we saw him after years of separation, this time as an American GI in Europe. (My brother Ernst became Ernest after he arrived in America).

10   Hostel Windermere, 1945:
     (top row, left to right) Sophie Goldschmidt, Elfi Reinert, Ruth Oppenheimer, Lisl Shearer (Scherzer). Lisl's father had his name changed from Viennese Scherzer to English Shearer when in the Pioneer Corps, hence the change in Lisl's name also.
     (middle row, left to right) Regina Gutwirth, Ruth Adamecz, Margot Hirsch, Lore Freitag, Hilde Roth.
     (bottom row, left to right) Inge Adamecz, Ruth Fisch, Lea Roth, Frieda (Friedchen) Roth.

Acknowledgements

With his permission, I have taken the title for this book from the oratorio by the late Sir Michael Tippett, a work I found deeply moving and relevant to my own experience when I first heard it performed by Leicestershire school pupils at the de Montfort Hall, Leicester, under the direction of the composer.

My thanks are due to my friend in Germany, Hilde Katzenmeier, for passing on my script to Renate Knigge-Tesche of the Landeszentrale für politische Bildung (Hessen), who organized its publication in German (1996), mainly for the benefit of German schools.

Friends and family have all encouraged me to write my memoirs, to help break the conspiracy of silence in which both perpetrators and victims have colluded for half a century. I very much appreciated the replies I had to my queries from my contemporaries in the Tynemouth and later Windermere Refugee Hostel. I thank in particular Anita Fellner (Pittsburgh), Lea Taub (London), Ruth Adamecz-Cohen (Israel), for taking the trouble to tell me their stories in detail. This was not easy for them.

I have been specially helped by Kathie Hawbaker of Ames, Iowa, without whose computer expertise I would have been helpless. With her loyal, quiet friendship she has encouraged and helped me enormously. Dr and Mrs Leroy Johnson of Ames provided the portrait photograph. Iradj Bagherzade of I.B.Tauris has helped with patient persistence, and my husband Herbert David has been unfailingly supportive. I thank them all.

1 From a small town in Germany

*A*uswanderung: 'emigration'. In German the word is vivid, less abstract than in English. *Aus*: 'out'; *wandern*: 'to wander'. When I was a young child this word was part of our daily vocabulary for as long as I can remember. The word frightened me. Where would we go? How would we wander? Like pilgrims? Like beggars? What could we take with us? What leave behind? I soon discovered that wherever we went it would not be a place where German was spoken. This I found particularly frightening. How would I ever learn to speak another language? How could I express my feelings, worries and fears in words other than German? With a child's certainty I knew it to be impossible.

Why emigrate? Decades later I know more than ever that no one emigrates happily or easily. The decision to leave for the unknown, especially for parents with family responsibilities, is horrendously difficult. A young man seeking adventure afar is not a real emigrant if he has the possibility of returning to a welcoming home. An emigrant, who is barred from returning, is a homeless refugee. The world today is full of wandering people who have fled their homes because they were persecuted, attacked, fearful, starving. Even in adverse conditions the temptation to stay in the place one knows is great. Lie low till the danger has passed. Better days will come. But sometimes the devil we know is even worse than the unknown and *Auswanderung* must take place.

The devil we had to face was Hitler. I was four years old when he came to power in Germany in 1933, so almost all my childhood memories are coloured by the fear and despair of that period. My life, and countless million other lives, were to be drastically altered or terminated by the *Führer*.

Our home was the village of Fränkisch-Crumbach in the Odenwald, a rural and pretty district of the *Land* of Hessen. Even today, to the uninformed tourist, Fränkisch-Crumbach is an archetypal example of what a German village should be. Each dwelling has grown individually according to the means or standing of its proprietor. Gardens still surround the red-roofed houses. The older ones are clad in the traditional local shingles, overlapping pieces of hand-cut wood, either pointed or round-ended and painted overall. Many of these homes were farmsteads in the old days. Some of the houses still display the gaping grilled apertures at ground level, where the cattle were kept. Families lived above and the main entrance is often reached by a flight of stone steps. There are still large rounded wooden entrance gates, space enough to let a laden haywain through into an inner farmyard. Nowadays these entries usually lead to a garage. There is a centuries old Gothic church, a manor house complete with a local baron, and the romantic ruins of an ancient fortress, Burg Rodenstein, nearby in a setting of hills, flower meadows, orchards and dark forest.

The Odenwald forests for me were closely interwoven with the fairy tales of the brothers Grimm, which I had heard as a young child and later read. I both loved and feared them, and more than half believed them to be real. I even thought I knew where Little Red Riding Hood may have met her wolf and where the Sleeping Beauty might be hidden. I would not have been surprised to have encountered the Hänsel and Gretel gingerbread house on one of our walks through the dense, scented, silent dark green woods.

There were few cars in my childhood years, the most common transport was still the horse and cart on the untarred village streets. Agricultural wagons, however, were taken to and from the fields by ox-teams. Horse droppings were immediately picked up by local house-owners, with the double benefit of cleanliness and a supply of garden fertilizer. The village was pervaded by a pungent smell of dung. Every farm had its own dung-heap, whose contents were carried to the fields in the appropriate season. Today the dung-heaps are no more, but the occasional whiff of cattle still hangs in the air.

I knew that my family was Jewish but did not at the time understand how this made us different from other people. We were part of the village. As children we played with the village children. My sister Hannah and I attended the *Volksschule* (elementary school) like all our contemporaries. Our father ran a cigar factory founded by his father in the last quarter of the nineteenth century.

Father was Moritz Oppenheimer (born in 1878), one of the numerous children of Isaak and Johanna Oppenheimer. Johanna, born Rohrheimer, came from a family long settled in Lorsch, also Hessen. This little town was famous for the manufacture of tobacco products. The Oppenheimers seem to have been thoroughly integrated. They were known, liked and respected, with many friends in the village. Father was an active member of the local council for 16 years, elected as a Social Democrat. Apparently he had innovative ideas. He helped to bring electricity to Fränkisch-Crumbach early in the twentieth century. He cared for the welfare of the community.

My grandfather had been born and raised in the village. His grandfather was probably the first Jew to arrive there at the end of the eighteenth century. Fränkisch-Crumbach, like much of the rest of the country, had been badly devastated during the Thirty Years War. The village counted only eight families at the end of those strife-ridden decades. Slowly newcomers came, including the occasional Jewish family.

With the name Oppenheimer it seems likely that my ancestor originated from the town of Oppenheim on the Rhine, which in the Middle Ages had a very large Jewish population. For the sake of mutual support and prayer in a hostile world, Jews, as a despised minority, had clustered together in cities throughout Europe in mediaeval days.

From time to time, to alleviate the harsh conditions under which the populace existed, the Church encouraged Jewish bloodletting. The tradition of legalized murder goes back at least to the Crusades, when heroic knights – English, French, German and others – on their way east along the Rhine towards the Holy Land indulged in the sport of killing Europe's infidels, the Jews. Committed in the name of Christianity, the slaughter was not a sin to be confessed, forgiven or repented.

My first inkling of actual and deliberate Jew-killing came when I had learnt to read. In the attic of our house there was a cache of books, which we discovered as children. Were the books there because they were discarded or because they were not meant for our eyes? I do not know, though parents should realize that hidden books are the ones most eagerly devoured. There I encountered a history book that related the crusades in vivid detail, with lurid pictures. It depicted dark-haired Jewish women with their hands raised in supplication, their children cowering behind them while a brave, helmeted, chain-mailed crusader, with a cross marked on his chest, raised his sword to kill the dangerous infidels. In the background there were flames, houses and people burning. Above was the symbol of the cross.

The English word 'crusade' is no longer as vivid as the German 'Kreuzzug', which means exactly what it says, 'procession of the cross'. The pictures and words were my first warning of danger. I dared not tell anyone. It was a fear I had to keep to myself. I could not face persuading my parents to reassure me that this was not true; I knew it was.

Later, at least six years later, in the North of England, when with my sparse English I began to understand what our history teacher was saying, she too spoke of the crusades as grand and heroic. My comprehension was as limited as my courage, and I lacked sufficient language to argue. Was it right to kill defenceless people? In the name of religion? I had early learnt my Ten Commandments, of which the most important still seems to me 'Thou shalt not kill'. Is there a religion that does not teach that? I hope today's teacher would be better informed and today's child less hesitant to question.

Even later, at London University, we read the 'Chanson de Roland' ('Song of Roland'), the first great French epic poem. At one point our hero relishes the spurting of infidel blood. In the essay I duly wrote I deplored the lack of true religious feeling and the glorification of killing. The professor found my opinions curious but was willing to accept them with her benign tolerance for eccentrics.

Because of periodic slaughter and persecution during and after the Crusades, Jews often looked for a haven in country districts. In German states they had to apply to the local baron, count or duke for residence permission. Some refused, but as these nobles had the right to levy a special tax, the *Schutzgeld* ('protection money'), many of them succumbed to the temptation of extra revenue. The new arrivals, fleeing the bloodshed of the cities, were glad to pay up in the hope of survival. As Jews they continued to pay more taxes than their Christian neighbours. Most German villages thus acquired small Jewish communities, and on the whole these co-existed peaceably with their neighbours. The Jewish residents found life safer in the smaller rural communities, though it was wise to keep a low profile. Fränkisch-Crumbach had a history of an easy, if not totally untroubled, relationship with its Jewish inhabitants. There are records of neighbourly quarrels about the fruit of a pear tree hanging over another's garden, the kind of disputes that have been in existence in all communities throughout the ages.

How did Jews earn a living? This was not easy. They were not allowed to own land. So farming in what was largely a peasant economy was not possible. They were not allowed to practise as craftsmen, who endured long apprenticeships and were rightly respected artisans. Craftsmen belonged to ancient guilds, which strictly excluded Jews, who were therefore unable to develop the skills required for a good livelihood. They were allowed to trade, particularly cattle, and many country Jews had to become cattle dealers.

Having found comparative safety in the country, the Jewish community of Fränkisch-Crumbach continued and multiplied during the nineteenth century in the same measure as their Christian compatriots. In the 1870s my grandfather Isaak Oppenheimer was responsible for building a synagogue in the village, a simple but sturdy house of God. A Jewish cemetery was established a few miles away in the neighbouring village of Reichelsheim. The Jews had settled there as in countless other villages of the Odenwald and throughout all of Germany.

In World War I, Jews joined the Kaiser's military forces in large numbers. Could they have felt the cause was right? Or was it to prove what good and patriotic Germans they were? Antisemitism was as rife in the army as elsewhere. My German soldier uncle, Louis Oppenheimer, sent home a postcard from the front depicting a bearded Russian Jew juxtaposed to a hairy Russian louse. The intention was presumably anti-Russian, as the Russians were on the enemy side, but there was the assumption that one could whip up greater antagonism if the word 'Jew' was added. The death rate of the German Jews in the Kaiser's army was the same as that of their comrades, the non-Jewish soldiers. In Fränkisch-Crumbach the war memorial of 1914–18 bears the names of the villagers fallen for the *Vaterland*, among them three Jewish soldiers, two Karlsbergs and one Oppenheimer (Simon). It is gratifying to see those names today. Because of the disgrace implicit in Jewish names, some World War I entries on German war memorials were effaced during the Nazi regime. Dead Jewish heroes might have challenged the current propaganda that Jews were cowards. Many German towns and villages lost all their Jewish inhabitants and blotted out their every trace by destroying the synagogues and cemeteries. A conspiracy of silence is still frequently observed, and little remains to tell today's generation of Germans that German Jews once lived among them.

After the First World War, Fränkisch-Crumbach, like the rest of Germany, went through the trauma and attendant hardships of defeat. There was hunger and insufficient employment. Isaak Oppenheimer's sons tried to run the cigar factory. Isaak and his wife, my grandparents, died within days of each other during the savage outbreak of the 'Spanish' 'flu in 1918, towards the end of the war, a disease that killed more people than even a savage war could achieve. Two Oppenheimer sons, Joseph and Louis, moved to the nearest city, Darmstadt. My father, with his older brother Gustav in the background, was in charge of the factory.

Gustav was severely handicapped; he had never walked, owing to congenital dysplasia of the hips. He did propel himself about, never setting his feet on the ground; he had learnt to swing his body along with the help of crutches, having developed powerful arms. He was well read and had acquired a library in which we loved to browse as children. He must have been intelligent and inventive, as he constructed a wheelchair contraption that could take him up and down the stairs. He was self-educated and wise, and never lacked visitors. We children relished the stories he told or read us, and adults enjoyed his conversation.

My father had married Klara Löwenstein from Rexingen. She died in the early twenties of a failed gall bladder operation, leaving him with three young children, Anni, Ernst and Werner. There was an oil portrait of Klara in our dining room, a beautiful but mysterious woman – mysterious only because we, the younger children, knew so little about her and were hesitant to question our half-brothers, whom we loved dearly and looked up to as our elders. Today I am surprised by this innate tact. After all, it was their mother's picture that revealed to me the awesome possibility that one might lose a parent before adulthood. This idea continued to haunt me. The word 'orphan' must always have sent, and probably still does, a chill fear through every child's mind.

Father married Margarete (abbreviated to Grete by friends and family) Krämer, who eventually had four children: the eldest, Hannah, then myself, Michael and finally Feodora, called Feo. I find it difficult to imagine what life was like for my mother when she arrived in the village, certainly a remote backwater at that time. She was a city woman, born in Mannheim (1892), later brought up in the then liberal city of Frankfurt. Her parents seemed to be part of Frankfurt society. Outings to the theatre and opera were a regular feature of their lives. Mother herself, with her younger sister Liese, attended the opera from an early age. This was partly because the Krämer parents had an *abonnement*, regular seats available for each opera. Those they considered dull, or not worth seeing again, the daughters attended. Aunt Liese and my mother saw so many performances of Weber's *Freischütz* that they knew it by heart!

The sisters Liese and Grete attended good schools. Liese eventually took a Fröbel training and directed what became an interesting and well-known kindergarten in Frankfurt. My mother decided she wanted to study mathematics at university. In Germany, as elsewhere, it was still uncommon in the first decade of this century for women to take up higher academic studies. To be eligible for a university place Grete had to face examinations of a more advanced level than the girls' school she attended could offer, so she transferred and was accepted by the boys' *Gymnasium* (academic secondary school) as the only girl. Few women pursued the rigorous discipline of mathematics in her day, but Mother studied at four separate universities for her degree: Frankfurt, Berlin, Jena and Heidelberg. Moving from university to university, as mediaeval scholars did, remained the pattern in Germany. She eventually took a post to teach mathematics in a school that had been set up in Kaunas, Lithuania, for Jewish girls, who until then had had little opportunity for any education. It was pioneering work.

How did my mother, from a city and cosmopolitan background, come to know and marry my father in a remote and backward village? I wish I knew. Were the families part of a network that organized marriages for the widowed and unmarried? What did she make of life in Fränkisch-Crumbach? As a sophisticated intellectual, better educated than her husband and the rest of the village community, it must have been a rude shock. With whom could she socialize and converse? I remember no sign of unhappiness in her surroundings. Nor do I recall her complaining about her situation. I know she disliked gossip and made this very clear. We learnt as children that tittle-tattle was not for us. Perhaps the village women had little else to offer as conversation. She liked to read, but there was no library available. Perhaps she bought the books or borrowed them from friends in Frankfurt. It was not difficult to travel to Darmstadt and Frankfurt, and she did have domestic staff. However, she had acquired a ready-made family who had been on their own and were not necessarily thrilled by her arrival.

According to local tales, the young now motherless Oppenheimer children were liked in the village, and pitied. Primitive stories about stepmothers abounded, the brothers Grimm had furnished horrors aplenty to the German public. A sympathetic worker in the factory asked Werner, the youngest, how he liked his new stepmother. He replied tentatively: 'I can't tell, she hasn't beaten me yet'.

Life must have become hard for Grete early on. Anni, the eldest child, contracted tuberculosis, a disease that was still quite common then. Much time, concern and money were spent to save her but she died at 19. I remember the day of her death when I was two years old. My older siblings dispute this and say I imagined it but I think it possible that the gravity of that day so impressed itself on me that I can still see her on what was, I suppose, her death bed. Many years passed before I could comprehend the extent of the losses sustained by my older brothers in their youth.

During those years of the late twenties and the early thirties, the whole of Germany suffered inflation, with attendant hardships on a scale hitherto unknown. Prices rose astronomically and eventually became meaningless. Father showed me some of the absurdly inflated figures on postage stamps in his treasured collection. A million marks! Mother told us how her father had cashed in a life insurance and had to bring the huge sum back in a wheelbarrow. By the time he reached home, it had lost all value. My family was no exception to the hardship faced by the country. It was not only inflation that caused us financial difficulties. Twofold medical and surgical expenses, including Swiss sanatoria, doctors, nurses and extra domestic staff, depleted my father's resources. This in turn affected the factory. Trying to keep it running became a constant struggle.

In 1933 Hitler came to power and the Nazi threat became a reality. Political opposition from the left was immediately and ruthlessly suppressed. Concentration camps were set up for all those who voiced objection. The churches had to pledge allegiance to Hitler. Both Catholic and Protestant obliged, though it took the latter a month longer. The judiciary did the same. Anyone who spoke out in opposition was sent to Dachau, Buchenwald or Sachsenhausen, the early concentration camps.

Anti-Jewish decrees started to be enforced. All Jews in government employ, civil servants, teachers at schools or universities, scientists in research laboratories, were to be summarily dismissed, without compensation or pension. Jewish musicians, of whom there were many, were no longer to perform publicly. Those who could, tried to emigrate. There was no public outcry in their defence. Their professional colleagues watched them depart, some with silent regret, some with approval, many with satisfaction. Even in the so-called upper echelons of the universities, medicine and the law, voices were not raised. The Jewish population lost colleagues and friends. Neighbours no longer knew them. Sometimes it was fear that made them turn aside, often it was a desire to be part of the Nazi mob, to belong to the powerful. Jews now became strangers, outcasts, pariahs. Their amazement and disbelief turned to terror. Justice was beyond their reach.

Auswanderung grew into a desperate and real need. Writers, philosophers, artists too, by no means all Jewish, left Germany. It created the greatest loss of an intellectual elite that any country has ever suffered. Many of these fugitives were fortunate, they found doors open to their talents. They enriched the music, art and theatre, as well as the centres of learning, of their hosts. If celebrities, they usually had the means to emigrate, and if not their friends abroad were willing to rescue and to help. Fame has compensations.

It was not so simple for the ordinary Jewish citizen to emigrate. There were problems of unemployment in many countries. There was fear of foreigners and not much sympathy for Jews or real understanding of Nazi policy. Antisemitism was not uniquely German. There were of course many individuals abroad who cared and worked to bring in the persecuted. There were religious and academic groups which tried to do the same, but governments were wary. We hear those in power today make pious noises about not interfering in a country's internal policies. Similar voices were making the same noises in the 1930s.

For would-be emigrants with capital, it was usually not too difficult to come to the USA or Britain. The rich always survive more easily. But even those who had once had a comfortable standard of living were soon impoverished. Most lost their livelihood quickly. Businesses were ruined, ordinary employees sacked. Many of the poor had to stay and die in the Holocaust. There were also those who felt they could not face exile, could not cope with a new life, new language and the new skills required. Some were too old or sick to be accepted elsewhere. Some were young and fit but would not leave elderly invalids. Suicide became common. There were the misguided ones who had survived World War I, had been decorated for their valour, and thought the Iron Cross would save them. They carried their medals to the death camps.

2 The drive to emigrate

The Oppenheimers spent hours at a time, then weeks that turned into years discussing their *Auswanderung*. Relatives and others from the Odenwald had decided on South America. It was possible to enter Paraguay, Uruguay and Argentina without too many resources. Immigrants to these underdeveloped countries were given acres that had never been cultivated and they could settle there. The aim was agricultural development of land, which would help the surge of the local and national economy.

This was to be our way out too. Our mother was enthusiastic, Father less so. He was no longer a young man, nor in first-rate health. It was decided that brother Werner would leave first, alone, as it was easier for individuals than for whole families to emigrate and immigrate. He would work the land, set up a farm and bring the rest of us over.

Werner was immediately apprenticed on a farm outside Fränkisch-Crumbach. I know now that the farmer, Adam Weidmann, was good and brave to take him on, to let him work and train him at a time when Jews were not welcomed in any employment. This farmer also sold us eggs later, when the local shops displayed notices saying, 'Juden ist der Eintritt verboten' ('Jews are forbidden entry here').

All this took years. Werner did not leave for Argentina till 1938. From a mischievous, fun-loving, jolly boy, he quickly took on responsible

11

manhood. He worked so hard, first for a master and then on his own. He had little spare time and did not allow himself the luxury of illness. His letters home were written in an encouraging tone, with the constantly reiterated longing for the family to join him soon. When sending a birthday letter to Mother he wrote 'this year in Argentina!' as his wish for her, adding semi-hopefully, 'Einmal wird es schon werden' ('It will happen one of these days').

Werner was the first to leave as a *Vorfahrer* (one who would travel before the others). His work was devoted to bringing out those left behind. He laboured. Nevertheless, he faithfully found time to write home, always concerned as to what was happening in Germany and how we were faring. He described how the only available transport was the horse, which meant an arduous journey every time he visited the immigration authorities to speed up our coming. He was to encounter bureaucracy in all its arbitrary power, sometimes helpful, more often ignorant and deliberately off-putting. He had many frustrating sessions, and tried to avoid complaining in his letters, but the disappointment often came through with, 'I can't understand why...what...where...?' Difficulties were constantly invented for Werner by the Argentinians and for us by the Germans.

It became clear that we had to clutch at any means of escape. My parents decided to apply for entry to the USA too, but found it difficult to obtain an affidavit for our large family with an elderly head of household. We were eventually put on the waiting list, the famous American 'quota'. It was the first important English word I learnt. This word, together with 'affidavit' and the Spanish 'llamada', our entry certificate to Argentina, were exotic terms that became part of our daily conversation. How we longed for them to become real. 'Quota' was especially vital. I knew it as our own number that would rise to the head of the list one day, and would enable us to feel the relief of departure, of flight. Our eldest brother Ernst was going to be our *Vorfahrer* to the USA. He had Löwenstein uncles there, brothers of his late mother, who were willing to provide him with the sought-after, precious affidavit, and he was working his way through the lengthy process necessary to effect his departure. Our quota number did eventually come up. But by then my parents were in a concentration camp, we children were scattered, and the USA was at war with Germany.

In the late 1930s, as life became more and more restricted, my parents made the hard decision that they would try and send their younger children away too, to places that would take them, preferably in Europe. Our parents wanted the reassurance that we were at least not overseas. Holland at the time was prepared to take children and to look after them in families or hostels. Holland was also the nearest foreign country to us in the Odenwald, at least a place we children could locate in the atlas. Hannah's and my name were duly put on a Dutch waiting list. When I discovered this I created a hysterical storm, sheer terror at the thought of leaving home, so that my parents withdrew my name and substituted my brother's, Michael. Michael was a year younger than I and much braver. He and Hannah had a remarkable spirit of adventure, which I lacked. They were always good companions and seemed content with this decision.

In the event, so many children were waiting to go to Holland that Hannah's and Michael's names did not surface before the outbreak of the war. It was a blessing. Had they gone to Holland they would have been rounded up with all the other refugee children during the German occupation and deported eastwards to the gas chambers. Few of the deported adults returned to Holland after the war, and virtually no children.

Our youngest sibling was born in 1934 at home. The three older children had arrived in hospital, Hannah and I in Frankfurt, Michael in Darmstadt. I do not know whether it was the new restrictions or lack of funds that meant a home confinement for the fourth. The baby was called Feo, after my grandmother Feodora Krämer (born Pappenheim). Oma (granny) had just committed suicide by throwing herself into the River Main in her home town of Frankfurt. We never knew exactly why, but from letters written at the time it was clear that the pressure on the Jews and her children and grandchildren was draining her strength and will. Suicide of the elderly was not unusual at the time, often committed to remove a potential burden from the next generation. It was the first time that I witnessed adult despair as I saw my mother grieve. As children we never knew that Grandmother had not died naturally. Not until 30 years later, in England, clearing Aunt Liese's papers after her death, did I discover Oma Feodora's death certificate.

My grandmother had belonged to a society in which Jews were integrated and unafraid. They felt they belonged to a cultured, civilized nation, and were proud to be part of it. Indeed many Jews were scarcely aware of their Judaism. I do not regret her suicide, nor the fact that my three other grandparents had died before I knew them. We, their descendants, are spared the anguish of many of my friends who carry in their mental picture gallery an image of elderly relatives huddled in a cattle truck, spending days without food or water, heating or clean air, perhaps with straw on the floor but no room to lie down and a bucket for public toilet use, as they jolted their way to death.

With little sister Feo none of us felt any sibling rivalry. She was too young for that and we adored her. She provided fun with spontaneous laughter. She was a great joy in our lives, always unafraid; she had no inkling of danger, did not know or care what *Auswanderung* meant, and was truly happy – always smiling, she followed us like a faithful puppy, agreeing to all we wished to do.

When we were no longer able to play outside, when our neighbours' children were forbidden all contact with us, we were thrown together on our own resources but had the bonus of an empty factory as our playground. Feo sometimes spoiled our games of hide-and-seek, as she always joyfully revealed hiding places by squealing in her puppy-dog way. We once dealt with that by telling her that we had a special place for her to hide and she should stay there till we came to fetch her. We then laid her on a shelf in a cupboard, closed its doors and continued our game. The trusting, angelic child simply did as we asked, stayed in claustrophobic darkness and was sweet when we graciously released her. Anyone else would eventually have told tales. Not Feo.

How did we become conscious of the Nazi regime in Fränkisch-Crumbach? The picture of the *Führer* was displayed everywhere, in schools, shops, offices, on hoardings and in private homes. Gradually more and more men appeared in brown uniforms. They walked stiffly and threw out their arms in the 'Heil Hitler' greeting, which they made to sound like a hostile bark. Soldiers with rifles, or else with spades over their shoulders, marched to military music through the village, singing Nazi songs which were meant to frighten us with threats of 'Jewish blood dripping from our knives' and proud declarations: 'Heute gehört uns Deutschland, morgen die ganze Welt' ('Today Germany, tomorrow the World').

The swastika was prominent on their armbands. It was visible everywhere: on all official communications, on postage stamps and on the ubiquitous flags. Those monstrous, threatening flags. Blood-red around a white circle on which the menacing, angular black swastika seemed to spin. Every house had to sport one. Not ours. As Jews we were forbidden such display, and the lack of flags helped to mark us. We became daily more estranged from the society we had always assumed was ours.

It was not only adults who postured in uniform. There was the Hitler Youth for boys and the BDM (Bund Deutscher Mädchen), its female equivalent. I so wanted to participate in their activities. I liked the idea of sport, songs and campfires and the implicit comradeship, but was forced to accept that I was not eligible.

Uniforms and flags figured in all the papers. In those pre-television days we had illustrated magazines which produced an endless variety on the theme of Hitler among brown- or black-shirted cohorts, usually with mass gatherings around him, always backed by enormous flags. When he was not addressing serried ranks, he was stroking a large dog or patting a child's head, inevitably blond. Today I still balk at uniforms and flags anywhere, their arrant nationalism, their implied superiority and their automatic exclusion of others, the lesser folk.

It was at this time too that the word 'Aryan' became part of current vocabulary. 'Aryan' meant good, upright, Nordic, blond, blue-eyed, fearless and German, a far cry from its original meaning, relating to the Asiatic tribes which had wandered westward thousands of years ago. Jews could not be 'Aryan', however good, upright, blond, blue-eyed etc. There were regular school classes on racial characteristics. Heads and noses were measured, colour of eyes examined, and contrasting pictures shown of singularly ugly Jews and outstandingly handsome 'Aryans'. Teachers seemed willing to teach their charges to look down on the inferiors. There were numerous Christian Germans, I realized, who did not fit the standard 'Aryan' image. The logical inconsistencies were bothersome for me, even at that young age.

I rarely played with dolls, but there was one to which I was particularly attached. She was a beautiful 'Aryan' doll, with long fair plaits and blue eyes. Although our father, as well as Michael and Feo, had clear blue eyes, Hannah's and mine were a mix of colours and not quite right for those times. As for my hair, I once asked Mother whether I too could have plaits. She said my hair was not suitable, it was too thick and curly. In a fit of pique I cut off my doll's shining golden braids.

In 1935, at the age of six, I joined Hannah at the village school. My sister had always been reasonably happy there, and I expected to enjoy it too. My teacher wore a brown uniform and expected us all to leap to our feet shooting out our right arm in the Hitler salute when he or any teacher entered the classroom. I knew my parents would not be keen for me to do this, but I need not have had any qualms. I was told not to salute; I was to remain seated. Every time the class leapt up, I hung my head in shame. I was different and I had to live with it.

Our world, once apparently safe, had collapsed. We realized that anything could happen, that neither one-time friends, nor neighbours, neither the representatives of authority nor the law itself, would protect us. It was a hard lesson for children. My peers at school did not attack me, but I had stones thrown at me on the way home. I was less frightened by the physical danger than by the thought that children I knew had the wish to do this to me and seemed to be exercising a right. Perhaps some parents may have urged restraint, but I understood enough to realize that I could not appeal to an adult for help.

Our immediate school problems were soon solved. Although many Jewish children could continue their schooling in state schools throughout Germany till 9 November 1938, the Odenwald was politically reactionary. It had taken to National Socialism very rapidly, and as early as 1935 the authorities made it clear that Jewish children were no longer wanted in their schools. What the headmaster said to my parents, whom he knew well, when he asked them to remove Hannah and me from the school I shall never know.

Everything was now clear. We were outcasts. I no longer wanted to be out of doors, life seemed too unsafe. Notices had gone up outside swimming pools, cinemas, skating rinks and other places of recreation and entertainment denying entry to Jews. My dream of swimming lessons was now impossible.

We had to play at home, but we did have an empty factory available, as business was failing for my father. We could run around in empty spaces, play hide-and-seek, and operate the simple pulley lifts from the yard to the upper floors. It was hard work pulling on the ropes and spooky to be a passenger. The lifts had neither doors nor lights. The special attraction for Michael and me was the warning at the loading base that it was 'streng verboten' ('strictly forbidden') to convey people in those lifts! They were to be used only for crates of tobacco. Michael and I relished our illicit pleasure.

Fränkisch-Crumbach had no daily paper. In the 1930s radios were not a common possession, but the village boasted a town crier, who appeared daily at noon with his handbell and the villagers were meant to listen. He stopped in the Allee, our road, not far from our home. It was he who had to repeat the Nazi line for all to hear and for many to believe. Behind him was the official village noticeboard where the local authority put up information for farmers, ratepayers etc. Prominent on this board were the broadly spread pages of the *Stürmer*, a party tabloid rich with cartoons of grossly featured Jews stealing from the poor, eating while others starved, displaying lecherous leers from bloated faces, enticing sweet little long-plaited 'Aryan' girls. The regular slogan at the top of the paper was 'Die Juden sind unser Unglück' ('The Jews are our misfortune').

I had to pass this noticeboard to visit Uncle Gustav and his sister, Aunt Ida, who lived in the old grandparental home attached to the factory in the Erbacherstrasse. The cartoons in the *Stürmer* terrorized me. I hated walking past that noticeboard. If I had taken a circuitous route I would have had to expose myself to the eyes of the more crowded centre of the village. That was an even greater hazard, so I determined I would rush by the board and not look. But I usually broke my promise to myself and stole a peek. Terror has its fascination for children.

Until the second half of the thirties, Fränkisch-Crumbach had possessed only a tiny cinema. This was to change. The local café proprietor bought the synagogue from the Jewish community. Due to continuing emigration, the community had shrunk and there were no longer the ten men required to hold a service (women did not count!). The synagogue was then converted into a cinema. Soon after that Jews were not allowed to cross its threshold. Cinemas were not for them.

3 To school in Höchst

I n 1935 a small Jewish school was opened in Höchst im Odenwald. The regional education authorities in Darmstadt apparently ruled that all children, even if undesirable, should be off the streets. So they swept through party objections to grant permission for a Jewish school to open.

Höchst had long had a settled Jewish community. There was a prayer meeting room by the middle of the eighteenth century. At the beginning of the twentieth century a large, new synagogue was erected in the centre of the little town. Two rooms at the back of the building were now to be our classrooms. Funds to create a real school were non-existent.

The principal of the school, Hermann Kahn, lived next door. He was a respected figure among Jews and Christians alike, an educated German, a musician with a deep love of German music. He had been the successful and popular choirmaster of the Höchst Singers and eventually the director of the Odenwald Choir. The Odenwald was rightly proud of this distinguished musical group. Hermann Kahn was also a scholar of Hebrew and religious studies. There being no rabbi in Höchst, Herr Kahn was in charge of services and the religious education of the children. He was one of the many German Jews who identified utterly with Germany, who loved the country and its culture, who could not imagine life outside Germany. He was to learn to change.

We were 35 schoolchildren of all ages, converging on Höchst from our distant homes. As the two rooms at the back of the synagogue did not give us enough space, we had to invade Herr Kahn's private premises. The school could not afford many teachers, and although Jewish teachers were available from among those the state had dismissed two years earlier, they could employ only a Herr Strauss and a Herr Seif full-time. Seif is like the German word for soap, 'Seife'. Poor Herr Seif was to endure much mockery for his name and his nervous mannerisms.

My mother also taught part-time at the school. Hannah and I did not view this situation with joy. We felt that school should be strictly divorced from home. Childhood brings absurd worries, and I spent hours agonizing over letting the word 'Mummy' slip out unintentionally. Yet when it inevitably did, no one seemed to mind. After all, they knew she was my mother.

We did not enjoy a 'good' or 'normal' education. We were kept occupied in a school setting without educational equipment, sporting or academic facilities, though we did have a few books. But at least we were spared the Hitler portraits, the Nazi flags, salutes and rhetoric. Best of all, we did not have to fear ill-treatment within the school.

I recall with deep mortification that I was very unkind to the only immediate classmate I had. She was Evi Krämer, small and very thin, the eldest child of a large and poor family. I remember quarrelling with her. She was older than I, but I was bigger and stronger and took advantage of this in a vicious way. Aged eight, I managed to push her to the ground and sit on her, feeling triumphant at the time. I was to wonder for years whether she had survived my unkindness and that of the world around her. She had not.

The poor had fewer chances of survival. A family without means could not emigrate, had to stay put till fate decided otherwise. Fate appeared for the Krämers in the uniform of the local police on a September day in 1942. Those Jews in Höchst who had not managed to flee to the cities of Darmstadt or Frankfurt, where some had hoped to find anonymity, had to assemble in front of the Rathaus (Town Hall). There they were loaded onto trucks and taken to Darmstadt, the nearest town, to be deported to the east. There was no escape. They were all known.

On that last day in the little town, the distraught Mrs Krämer, a young widow, with her four daughters and their pathetic bundles, had said she wanted to hurry back to her house to collect the shoes of the youngest and some food she had left on the table. One of the men who was loading the victims for transport to Darmstadt and trying to avoid panic, was heard to say to her, 'Don't worry, you won't need those where you are going'. He knew what was to follow. This journey was to be their last. But if he knew, the others must have known too. So why such blank ignorance after the war?

From Darmstadt on 24 September 1942, the Krämer family with the others, old and young, left in cattle trucks for Auschwitz. I have not been able to shake off the memory of my unkindness to Evi Krämer. I hope that aged 14, she and her sisters Betty (10), Ruth (8) and Ilse (6), died quickly.

We did not all die. Many of my Höchst school companions were saved, but they are scattered throughout the world. Not one of the survivors has returned to live there.

Meanwhile we had our new school. For children in more outlying villages the journey there proved too far or too expensive and their education ceased. We were therefore supposed to consider ourselves fortunate, but hostility and harassment on the way to and from school made me long to stay at home. Some children were able to travel by train, as there was a rail link to their little towns, but those of us from Fränkisch-Crumbach and the next village, Reichelsheim, were taken in a large old van. Its normal seating had been replaced by rough wooden benches on which we children perched. It was a tough journey in snowy weather; we were stuck at times and could not find help. Occasionally the van broke down. Once, as we were coming down the hill approaching the village of Höllerbach, our brakes failed. Unfortunately a flock of sheep was coming up towards us. Poor Herr Seif – a troop of terrified children inside and a similar, uncontrolled mass of sheep outside – what could he do? He tried to avoid the sheep but still killed three of them. I can understand the farmer's anger, but this turned into a furious attack on Herr Seif. The accident had been caused by 'Jewish criminals'. There was much shouting and threatening language directed at us all. A nasty experience. Ever after, I dreaded going through Höllerbach. The village and its name became a symbol of terror, not least perhaps because I was conscious of language from an early age and the word 'Hölle' is German for hell.

Stones were thrown at our van, called the 'Jew bus', in most villages that we had to cross. Worse was to come later. By 1938, not long before the school finally closed, attacks on Jews had become more common-place. We were on the whole cheerful children: we often sang on our way and joked with each other. One day, when we seemed to have nothing to fear, we saw in the distance a stationary lorry at right angles across the road. Herr Seif must have been puzzled. He had to stop. My mother and the Oppenheimer children recognized the lorry. It belonged to a haulage firm in Fränkisch-Crumbach. It was so easy to identify. I can see it today, dark blue with a pattern of white diamond shapes running around the carrier. The owner was Herr Keil, and there he was. He got down from his cab, a starting handle in his fist. He came towards us. Without a word, he proceeded to smash the windows of our van, behind which we children screamed and cowered. Why did he do this? Had his colleagues in the party suggested it? Did he know he would derive pleasure from terrorizing young children? Was he going to brag to his drinking companions about this personal triumph over the Jews, as the men enjoyed their evening beer? Did anyone voice an objection?

It was another first for me. I had not seen an adult man afraid before. Poor, helpless Herr Seif. This was not the last of his ordeals. During the Kristallnacht of November 1938 he was brutally beaten in his home town of Reichelsheim. He eventually fled with his family to Frankfurt, but there was no further hiding place when they came to seize him, his wife and three little children for transport to Auschwitz. They all perished there, the youngest barely four years old.

Another new lesson that day was that a parent cannot always come to one's rescue. Till then, there had never been a time when Mother was not available to help us in our distress. Surely that was the reason for her existence? There is still a vivid picture of her in my memory: sitting next to the driver, she was looking straight ahead, her face rigid.

After that I did not want to go to school any more. I do not think the term 'school phobia' had reached the Odenwald, but all of us had the same fears. However, we had to pretend that life was normal and there-fore continue our trek to Höchst, though somewhat spasmodically. I was

not the only one who fabricated aches and pains and found ways to avoid the hazardous journey to school.

Over 40 years later I was to meet Herr Keil again. His amiable son, whom I encountered by chance as I bought petrol from him, had been delighted to discover my identity on my brief visit to Fränkisch-Crumbach. He introduced himself to me. The name suddenly raised alarming memories and when he smilingly said 'You must come in and see my father,' I tried to resist, but young Herr Keil took my hand and dragged me along to meet an old, dispirited, gloomy-looking man. The son introduced me excitedly, 'Father, do you know who this is? It's Ruth Oppenheimer!'

Hearing my name, the old man said, 'I don't know you'.

I am sure that was true. Feebly I replied, 'I am a daughter of Moritz Oppenheimer who had the cigar factory up the road'.

He did not react. I left the room as quickly as I could.

4 At home in Fränkisch-Crumbach

T oday, when I read of all the measures taken against the Jews during those early Nazi years, I realize that our parents must have made great efforts to shield us. We were isolated, admittedly, but we still seemed to lead a good family life. As a child, I did not hear about the Nuremberg laws. They related to blood. The purity of 'Aryan' blood, the inferior blood of the Jews. The horror of miscegenation. This of course led to the difficult question of how to define a Jew, how many Jewish grandparents had tainted that blood. It was possible to remain a good German with only one Jewish grandparent, provided he or she had been a non-practising Jew. Intermarriage was strictly forbidden, as were sexual relationships between Jews and non-Jews outside matrimony. Female Christian domestic staff under 45 were no longer permitted in Jewish homes, the Jewish male being untrustworthy. Jewish doctors could not treat non-Jews, and eventually non-Jews could not work in Jewish enterprises. I understood that Jews were no longer able to vote, but at the time I could not comprehend the loss of other civil and human rights. As Jews did not pay subscriptions to the Nazi Party they had a special tax levied upon them instead. Gradually even sheltered children could feel the petty restrictions as well as the major humiliations.

One of these, though quite exciting and novel for us children, was the acquisition of new names. This caused hilarity for the young, though we felt the disquiet raised in the adult mind. In Germany, as in other continental European countries, Old Testament names such as Hannah, Rachel, Ruth, David, Jonathan, Jacob, were more widely, though not exclusively, used by Jews rather than Christians. In the USA and Great Britain, on the contrary, biblical names, whether from the Old or New Testament, have always been popular. Some Jews had very Germanic names – they were after all Germans and as proud of their German history as anyone else, so it was not unusual to have Siegfrieds and Hermanns and other Teutonic heroes in Jewish families. An order went out that Jews were no longer allowed to hide their identity behind such noble names. A list was drawn up of those they might use. Men were allowed the names 'Abel, Abieser, Abimelech, Abner, Absalom, Ahab, Ahasja' to 'Zadek, Zedekia, Zephanja, Zeraja, Zewi'. Some of these were obviously more arcane than others. Females had a more restricted choice, from respectable (to Anglo-Saxon ears) 'Abigail', followed by 'Baschewa, Beile, Bela, Bescha' through to 'Zerel, Zilla, Zimle, Zipora, Zirel, Zorthel'.

If Jews did not happen to own a name on that list, and most of them did not, then all male Jews had to append 'Israel' to their official names, all women had to add 'Sara'. This was to ensure that documents and letters pertaining to Jews could be immediately identified. If Jews did not use the new full name every time a signature was required, they were to be punished. The new law stated, 'He who does not give his first full Jewish name in legal or commercial dealings will receive a sentence of up to six months imprisonment'. At the same time the new directive suggested that German citizens (Jews had lost their nationality) should use only true German names for their progeny, preferably ancient and Germanic, that had been used in previous generations to indicate their 'Aryan' links. Foreign names might be used only when the authorities approved. I did not really mind the indignity of the extra name personally, thinking 'Ruth Luise Sara' was abundance in a part of the world where even two first names were ostentatious. From my reading I knew that only the nobility could allow themselves such extravagance.

We had been part of the general melee of children who played the outdoor seasonal games in the street. This was taken for granted by us and our contemporaries. Most of us country dwellers had gardens. These were arranged into tidy flower, but more importantly vegetable, beds and were not to be carelessly trampled on in childish pursuits. If we wanted to play tag, and we did, the streets were available, real traffic non-existent. It was easy enough to make way for the horses and carts that rumbled along, and the ox-wagons lumbered at even slower speeds. A real motor car was cause for excitement and jubilation.

Like the other children, we knew instinctively when the marble season was on, when to get out the spinning tops and whips, when to whizz down the untarred, bumpy road on our scooters. The height of ambition was to graduate to a bicycle. Hannah, Michael and I were part of the crowd. Once we were expelled from school, all contact ceased with our erstwhile playmates. They too had learnt that we were undesirable, even targets for insults and worse.

Hannah and Michael each had a special friend, a neighbouring child of their own age. Hannah's friend was Heinrich Hartmann, who lived next door. For years they played together, the one always available for the other. They got up to all sorts of pranks, mainly harmless mischief, though sometimes dangerous to the adult eye, as when, for example, they decided to explore the hayloft – which was *verboten* – via a high and totally vertical ladder. On another occasion they both appeared with wide grins, having decided to swap clothes, and it took a moment or two for us all to realize what they had done. The adults tried to disguise their laughter, and declared their disapproval. We, the younger children, full of admiration for their daring inventiveness, laughed till it hurt. One day the friendship ceased. Heinrich was in his yard and Hannah called to him as usual. He disappeared round the corner and never played nor spoke with her again. Had the Hitler Youth leader forbidden it? Or his parents? But then they too no longer communicated with us, their neighbours. The loss of Heinrich hit Hannah hard.

Helmut Schneller in the house across the road was a devoted friend of Michael's. They too had played together, in the street as well as in each other's houses. They shared their toys and their small boys' mischief. Helmut's grandfather had always worked in the factory, and there had been a mutual neighbourly understanding. One day, however, Helmut's father appeared in the brown Nazi uniform with a swastika armband. Michael, a year younger than I, did not appreciate the significance, nor did he understand why Helmut would not longer play with him. I was quite aware of Herr Schneller's frown and his angry looks in our direction. To make matters worse, Helmut had just acquired his first bicycle, on which of course Michael was longing to take a turn. Instead, hiding behind our sitting-room curtains, he watched little blond Helmut, his head held high, cycling up and down in front of our house. This friendship too came to an abrupt end.

Forced to remain indoors, we were obliged to find our own entertainment, and we read. I do not know where the books came from, there always seemed to be plenty in the house. There was no library in Fränkisch-Crumbach. If there had been, *Juden* would have been *verboten*. Learning to read must have been a relatively simple process for me, as I do not remember it. German is after all a phonetic language and literacy is a greater problem for anglophones. My sister Hannah was my example. I constantly tried to vie with her and must have been a nuisance. She read whenever, wherever and whatever she could seize. I followed, not by any means always understanding what I read. Hannah was probably the only one to see through my pretence, and challenged me. I am sure I protested and lied loudly. I am grateful for the example she set.

Meanwhile, talk of *Auswanderung* never ceased. While in theory I realized that we had to leave our *Heimat*, a very evocative word to Germans, a combination of home, hearth and country, I became aware of the fact that we would have to learn a new language. Wherever we went in the Western Hemisphere, German would not be the vernacular. I had become defeatist early in life, and knew that I was incapable of acquiring a foreign language. The language that frightened me was not English, but Spanish. We were going to need Spanish in Argentina, that very distant country to which we intended to emigrate. We often looked at the map to see where brother Werner was, and there seemed to be so much deep sea to cross! Other exotic and mysterious names had cropped up, Uruguay and Paraguay, and indeed cousins disappeared to both these states from our small community in Germany. My distress was partly because I realized that I would be deprived of the pleasure of reading. How could one possibly read, let alone enjoy, books in Spanish or English? Such literature was bound to be less good than our German variety. Little did I realize that the *David Copperfield* (simplified, I think), *Tom* (Sawyer) and *Onkel Toms Hütte* which I wept over and adored had been in English in the original.

Slowly there were more anti-Jewish decrees. As children we did not comprehend the significance of some of these when they pertained to withdrawals of human rights, or the imposition of special taxes. We could not help, however, witnessing the removal of the cutlery that we had known and used daily. Jews were no longer allowed to own valuables in the form of silver (cutlery) and jewellery. It had to be handed over to the local Nazis. Our parents, being honest, did as they were told. Our property was willingly accepted. Aunt Liese, single and without children, was less compliant and I feel proud of her today. She said that if she was going to give away the inherited family silver she would prefer the recipients to be of her own choice. Brave woman. She gave it to friends in the town of Ulm (Southern Germany), telling them that it was a gift, she would not want it back, and they were to think of it as theirs.

Aunt Liese eventually found refuge in England on a domestic work permit. Women on their own were allowed to migrate to England on condition that they took only domestic cleaning jobs, for which of course they were paid very little. She had a hard time, but survived on her very low income. Not long after the end of the war, a brown paper parcel festooned with much string arrived in York. My aunt was overwhelmed. The friends in Ulm, in very straitened circumstances at the end of the war, had sent her the silver cutlery. In spite of all that she had experienced and endured under the Nazis, Aunt Liese lived and breathed German art, music, literature and theatre. Ever afterwards, this cutlery was known as the 'Rheingold' or the 'Treasure of the Nibelungen'. She left this cutlery to my brother Michael and me. I treasure my share of it. It is a constant reminder and a witness to the potential for goodness in humans.

Mother started to learn Spanish, from a book. She had not studied languages but had a reasonable knowledge of French and English and did not feel daunted by the idea of Spanish. Werner wrote very positive letters from Argentina, and clearly had learnt Spanish and impressed us with words like 'gaucho'. The idea of emigration was treated positively. Hannah and Michael looked on it as something of an adventure. I think I was the only negative Oppenheimer. Apart from the language which I knew I could not master, I was repelled by the thought of having to do the milking, a daily essential chore and most likely to be done by the young. I was frightened of cows. Though merely afraid of cows, I was actually terrified of horses, and it was clear that if we were to go to school, or anywhere else, it would be on horseback. I wept, I complained. I was afraid of horses, though I knew they did not personally loathe me. The Nazis did.

Although we were unable to mix socially with Christians, we still occasionally visited our relatives in Frankfurt, Mannheim and Hanau. Those outings were a treat. I remember going to the university town of Heidelberg with Mother. She spoke exuberantly of her student days there. And now the notices told Jews to keep out. As we passed the university buildings, long the seat of education and *Kultur*, with their great scholars, researchers and professors, my mother would fall silent, staring straight ahead with a faster pace to her stride.

And the relatives we visited? They all spoke of *Auswanderung*. Where to? How? Everyone was trying to leave. In Hanau we went to see great-uncle Leopold Oppenheim. His wife Olga, Grandmother Feo's sister, had been badly injured in a tram accident and died young. Their daughter Lotte looked after him and the household. She had been unable to have any professional training. It was taken for granted that an unmarried daughter would remain single and look after her widowed father. As a well brought up young lady, she had learnt to play the piano, her only skill. Another sister, Annie, had married. In the spring of 1939 great-uncle Leopold persuaded Lotte to leave for London. As a single woman she too was able to enter Britain with a domestic permit, on condition that she did nothing else. So she became a cleaning woman and cleaned and sometimes cooked for Londoners throughout the war and the air raids. Her wages were very low. Lotte continued to live in London well into old age, but remained deeply unhappy. One day she was sent a newspaper from Hanau. In it was a picture of her former elegant home, now an elegant hotel.

5   The cigar factory

With all the new regulations, anti-Jewish laws that seemed to increase daily, life – that is earning a living – became nightmarish and often impossible.

As a child, I did not know what was happening to Father's work, though I knew he was anxious and troubled and constantly making an effort, which entailed writing, phoning and travelling. I do not think my older siblings knew much more. My parents must have tried so hard to spare us. It was clear that money was short, that clothes were handed down, repaired and adjusted, that food must never be wasted. But money had to be spent on expensive postage for the many letters that were sent abroad in the hope that we would find anchor somewhere.

The slump, the crash of 1929 and the depression had affected Father and his work, as they had affected many other Germans. His cigar factory had ceased to function. He tried hard to revive the operation, and there seemed to be a time when there were women working in the factory, cheerful and friendly to us children. But I remember a longer period when the factory stood empty. Father's fate and that of the factory, although we did not realize it early enough, had been decided by the advent of Hitler. With hindsight it is easy to see that there never would be any help, but at the time Father persevered and made every effort to resuscitate the business. He too knew that we must emigrate, but felt daunted by the enormity of such an undertaking. He knew no language but German, he had spent most of his working life on one project, the factory and the welfare of his personnel. It was Mother who saw the urgency more clearly and who, 14 years younger than her husband, was more prepared to face a new and probably very hard life. He still hoped that normality would return to Germany, the only country he knew and had loved.

Father was to endure the same harsh measures that now affected all Jewish enterprises. His fate is described in the correspondence of the Fränkisch-Crumbach Council,* which today still makes sad and bitter reading, but the actual experience for my father must have been desperate.

After all, Jewish civil servants had been dismissed from their jobs; that included everyone in state or national employment as early as 1933. Now it was the turn of Jewish businesses. Supplies were stopped for manufacturing. In my father's case, he could no longer obtain the required tobacco to keep his workers busy. Non-Jews were supposed to cease working in Jewish concerns. This was hard on the Crumbacher workers who had little other employment available. To prevent this happening a new law was brought out, not only for our factory but for every business owned by Jews. All enterprises belonging to Jews were to be *arisiert* ('aryanized'). An 'Aryan' had to take charge of the firm, or at least accompany the existing director or manager with a view to taking over. To make clear what 'aryanization' meant, a new word was invented. German is a splendidly creative language. This was *Entjudung* ('removal of Jews'). When this was not sufficient, a better word came up: *Zwangsentjudung* ('enforced removal of Jews'). The *Bürgermeister* of Fränkisch-Crumbach, Herr Trinkaus, informed Father of this new decree. In June 1934 he demanded that henceforth all factory correspondence and business dealings required the extra signature of a 'person of Aryan descent'.

The mayor had another function in life. He was the leader of the local Nazi party, the NSDAP, a job that carried more honour than the running of the village. He proved to be a Nazi worthy of his *Führer* in

---

* The correspondence on my father has survived by chance, although in the last days of the war Hitler had ordered that all documents pertaining to Jews should be burnt. It is in the archives of the Rathaus in Fränkisch-Crumbach.

Nationalsozialiſtiſche Deutſche Arbeiterpartei

Gau   Heſſen-Naſſau

Gaugeſchäftsſtelle:		Kampfzeitungen des Gaues:
Frankfurt/Main, Gutleutſtr. 8—12, Schließfach 1636		„Frankfurter Volksblatt" Frankfurt/Main
Girokonto 6221 Naſſauiſche Landesbank, Frankfurt am Main		Neue Mainzerſtraße 8, Fernſprecher 28232
Fernſpr.: Sammelnummer: 30381		„Heſſiſche Landeszeitung" Darmſtadt
Poſtſcheck-Konto: Frankfurt/Main 83003		Rheinſtraße 22 — Fernſprecher 2445

Kreisleitung Dieburg   Dieburg, den 16. Dezember 1936.

Abteilung:Kreisleiter
Ga/Ra.

An die

Ortsgruppe der NSDAP
Ortsgruppenleiter T r i n k a u s
F r ä n k. - C r u m b a c h
Kreis Dieburg.

Betrifft: Die Cigarrenfabrik Krämer & Co., Fränkisch-Crumbach.

Das mir überlassene Schreibendes Dr. jur. Karl Warthorst, Treu-
händer, an die Bank für Deutsche Arbeit, übersende ich Ihnen bei-
liegend wieder zurück, und gebe Ihnen meine Stellungnahme wie folg
bekannt:

Da anzunahmen ist, dass die Firma Krämer & Co. die Fortsetzung
der Firma J. Oppenheimer Söhne ist, die schon mehrere Vergleiche
geschlossen hat d.h. ihre Gläubiger ums Geld brachte, wird der
Antrag der Firma Krämer & Co. von mir abgelehnt.

Meines Erachtens ist es ein Unding, einer jüdischen Firma ein
Darlehen aus den Spargroschen der deutschen Volksgenossen oder
aber aus Mitteln des Staates zu gewähren, da aufgrund der früheren
Geschäftsgebaren zu befürchten ist, dass die Juden auf irgendeine
Art und Weise doch wieder ihre Betrügereien weiter treiben.
Für uns Als Nationalsozialisten dürfen wir hier nicht wegen einigen
Arbeitslosen unsere Prinzipien aufgeben um so mehr, da seit 1933
doch schon 80% der s.ztg. Arbeitslosen untergebracht sind und die
restlichen noch in Arbeit gebracht werden.

Heil Hitler !

Höflichkeitsformeln fallen bei allen parteiamtlichen Schreiben weg.

his virulent hatred of my father and presumably of all Jews. He followed the given party line.

He wrote to Dieburg, then a type of county town and the nearest higher authority, telling them that he wanted work for the otherwise unemployed of Fränkisch-Crumbach, but that he did not want my father to profit from such work. He praised the workers, saying they had 'a good attitude to our state', and added that they were all party members.

In his letters Herr Trinkaus used the pompous language of the time, garnished with swastika stamps and the inevitable 'Heil Hitler!' greeting. My father's letters did not use that greeting, but all ended with the enforced new signature, 'Moritz Israel Oppenheimer'.

Writing to the authorities in Dieburg, Herr Trinkaus makes it clear quite early on that the community would benefit if my father were not merely accompanied by an 'Aryan' co-director, but removed altogether: 'Surely the Oppenheimer firm is now finished and each day's delay means further damage to the German economy at the hands of a Jew'. Herr Trinkaus even proposes that the village could sell the factory and auction off all Oppenheimer property and belongings for local benefit. He has a list of what we owned in the way of furniture and other effects. (He did not know then, but may have had an inkling, that we would be driven out of the place and dispersed, and that anything we had owned would be available.) In his earlier letters the mayor would refer to my father as Herr Oppenheimer; later the courtesy title is dropped and he becomes Oppenheimer. Finally, he is just 'the Jew', a creature obviously to be despised. It is therefore easy for him to say, 'I must assume that the Jew is lying to me'.

He is torn by conflicting desires. He would like the factory to be operative, so that local workers might earn a living, but at the same time he would like to be rid of my father: 'It is my view that in the interests of the local workforce the business must be re-started, but the Jew as a Jew cannot have any support'.

Herr Trinkaus goes on to reflect the attitudes of Nazis in more elevated places: 'I have made it my goal to drive out all the Jews from our community and do not intend to attract Jews here'.

The *Bürgermeister*'s plan was clear. He wanted the factory, but the Jews were to be driven out. In pleading for help for the workers, he has

Moritz Israel Oppenheimer   Mannheim 27 November 39

Mannheim R 7. 24

Telephon 26992

Herrn

Bürgermeister Trinkaus

Fränk- Crumbach i/Odenw.

       Philipp Jungblut rief mich gestern Früh an & wollte mic
nochmal überreden ihm die Wohnung in der Fabrik zu überlassen. Ich
habe ihm lt. beiliegendem Durchschlag geschrieben. Im Laufe dieser
Woche will ein Zigarrenfabrikant Hediger von Hier mit einem Vermit
aus Bensheim nach dort kommen um die Fabrik zu besichtigen, dersel
wird sich wohl auch mit Ihnen in Verbindung setzen. Von Herrn Dopf
habe keine Nachricht erhalten. Für Ihre Bemühungen sage Ihnen noch
meinen besten Dank & zeichne   Hochachtend

Moritz Israel Oppenheim

the honesty to say, 'It was only the flourishing cigar industry that once gave our workers a good living'. But he did not say who had provided it. There is, however, a scribbled pencil note among the papers, in old gothic script, though I cannot be sure that it is Herr Trinkaus's handwriting: 'Der Jude muss erledigt werden' ('The Jew must be finished off').

Father eventually tried to sell the factory, seeing that as the only solution to finding enough money to permit us to pay for the expensive boat passage to Argentina. People knew that there was a 'Jewish' factory for sale. (No one ever spoke of a Catholic or Protestant factory in Germany.) Some interest was shown, but Herr Trinkaus, who was always involved, must have made it clear that eventually one could have the place for nothing. He did not wish my father to draw any profit from what had been family property, and a benefit to the community: 'I have no interest in seeing the Jew with money left'.

Herr Trinkaus threatened to write to the passport office to ensure that no passports would be issued to the Oppenheimers. This may or may not have been done.

But the mayor was not my father's only enemy. Other correspondence from that time reciprocated Herr Trinkaus's attitudes. In response to the mayor's plea that work should be available for the faithful factory workers, now all party members, a higher official of the NSDAP writes, 'It would be monstrous to grant a Jewish firm a loan from the pennies saved by our German compatriots ... as we have cause to fear from earlier experience, that the Jews in some way or other will continue to cheat'.

Similarly, my father's lawyer, with whom he had dealt for years, Dr Warthorst of Darmstadt, wanting to declare himself part of the new regime, wrote to the Bank for German Work in Frankfurt asking for a loan to revitalize the factory. He explained that this was to give bread and work to some workers but also secondarily to ensure that the factory could be sold and 'elevated to "Aryan" ownership'.

Father had trusted him in the past. Dr Warthorst, perhaps aware of his disloyalty, closed his letter to the mayor with the following words: 'Please treat my writing with confidentiality'.

The difficulties did not cease. Father had been forced to sell the large, solid family house he had built in the Allee when he married Klara Löwenstein. The house was clearly too good for us. It was sold at well below its value. What right had we to expect a fair price? We moved into the old house attached to the factory, where the grandparents had lived with their family and where our much loved physically handicapped Uncle Gustav had continued to live with his sister, mentally disturbed Aunt Ida. We were fortunate. Many others who had to leave their good homes had nowhere to go, had to split up their families and hope for a charitable corner somewhere.

Less than a year later, the family had to face the horrors of Kristallnacht, and my father the concentration camp Buchenwald. We were forced out of the village, as life had become impossible. The aunt and uncle eventually found shelter of limited duration in a Jewish old people's home in Worms. The house and factory stood empty. A local inhabitant, Herr Jungblut, wanted to buy it, and agreed with Father on a low price. The mayor stopped this, saying, 'The Jew was demanding a senselessly elevated price'.

After the war, there was no criticism of Herr Trinkaus's behaviour. He had performed his duties well, one of which was the hounding of my father. He had been a caring mayor. His picture appears in the local museum among other mayors who are honoured and recognized. When he died, there was a splendid funeral attended by almost all the inhabitants of Fränkisch-Crumbach.

6 Mina

A n important member of our household was Mina, the *Dienst-
mädchen* ('maidservant'). This was her job description in the
terminology of the day, but she was much more than that. She
ran the household, looked after us, gave orders to everyone and did not
like to hear the word 'no'. She shared the cooking with Mother, did the
gardening with some of us, and frequently gave her opinion of individual
family members, by no means always flattering.

Mina and I had a special bond. Because brother Michael's birth took
place 364 days after mine, and Mother had to give first care to the new
baby, I became Mina's child and she looked after me devotedly. She spoiled
me. The others were aware of this, as I was. If there was a quarrel with any
of the siblings she would take up my cause without prior investigation.
I of course took full advantage of this.

Mina was not only devoted to us. As a good Catholic she was devoted
to her church. Fränkisch-Crumbach has a thirteenth-century church
that had of course been Catholic before the Reformation but has been
Protestant since. Catholics were almost non-existent in the village in
my time. Today there is a modern Catholic church built for the post-
war influx of Sudetenland refugees, ethnic Germans expelled from
Czechoslovakia after the German defeat in 1945.

The few Catholics in the village before that influx were prominent people, in my day none other than the local baroness and her family, who lived in the manor house surrounded by a splendid park in the middle of the village. In addition to a fine house, this ancient family had its own small church in a secluded corner of the park. The baroness and her servants attended mass there, and in an uncharacteristically democratic way the few local village Catholics were invited to the church.

Mina was a regular attender. So was I, though less regular. I knew that Mother did not actually want me to go to church with Mina, but really she had little say in the matter. If I wished to go, Mina would take me. I understood little of the service. It was in Latin. As the service in the synagogue was in Hebrew, this other unknown language did not seem so odd. I knew both services were to praise God, and the Catholic Church to me as a six-year-old was very much more attractive. There were pictures; in the synagogue the walls were bare. There was music. In the synagogue there was singing but the ancient unaccompanied chants were deeply sad. There was a wonderful smell in the Catholic Church. I had the idea that the smell was part of its natural beauty; I was unacquainted with incense until I was much older. And there were candles. The synagogue was austere in comparison.

Best of all were occasional festivals. I remember the feast of the Assumption best. The German name for that is again so much more picturesque. After all, what does 'Assumption' mean to most people? 'Maria Himmelfahrt' – 'Mary's ride to Heaven' – conjures up at the very least visions of Cinderella in a golden coach. I remember little girls dressed in white muslin, scattering flower petals. What could be more romantic, more sentimentally appealing? I had no wish to be one of those little girls, but I was glad to witness something so gentle and beautiful. I understood quite early that I was not meant to be part of this scene. There was a crucifix, which frightened me. Who told me that the Jews had killed Jesus? I do not know, but I did understand that I was connected with that death and in some way responsible. It was a heavy burden. I knew I was innocent but sensed that others believed me guilty.

Mina, who had little education, loved us in spite of our non-membership of the Christian community. She clearly could not think of us as different. She had the peasant woman's common sense. In spite of what she must have been taught at Sunday school, she did not blame us for the death of her Saviour as so many Christians did. She had strong beliefs; she knew there was a heaven and a hell with angels and devils. And she was brave, loyal, good.

When the local party minions came to collect her to vote for the Nazis, Mina gave them such a caustic scolding that they slunk away. When the order came out, via the town crier, that 'Aryans' were no longer allowed to work for Jews, she shrugged her shoulders and ignored what she considered a stupidity. When Father tried to send her away (difficult, as she had no other home), she refused to leave. Eventually she had to go, a tearful occasion. I could not come to terms with her leaving. It was my first inkling of what the death of a loved one might be.

She had cared for me and loved me, and I loved her devotedly in return. I was slowly beginning to understand what genuine injustice was. When, some months later, the family moved to Mannheim for the anonymity and the work that Mother found there, Feo and I had to be left behind because we were sick with whooping cough. Mother was going to direct the Jewish orphanage in Mannheim. In those days it was considered an act of quasi-criminality to bring an infectious sickness into a house of children. Whether we liked it or not, Feo and I were forced to stay in Fränkisch-Crumbach. We lived in quarantine with Uncle Gustav and Aunt Ida, who were not capable of looking after themselves at the time, let alone us. So Mina, who never lost touch, came back, strictly against Nazi orders. I think the local guardians of the law were too scared of her to intervene. She bought food for us in the shops we were not allowed to enter. She looked after and comforted two very frightened little girls.

I heard only recently, that Mrs Trinkaus, the *Bürgermeister*'s wife, was willing to sell milk secretly to Mina. Why would she do this? And did her husband know?

Mina continued to stay in touch with my parents. She came to see them. It was a punishable offence to be *judenfreundlich* ('friendly to Jews'). She must have been a comfort to them in a world from which they had lost all their non-Jewish friends, where the ordinary population was entitled to commit random hostile and brutal acts.

I do not understand the Church's process of beatification. But Mina Dümig was certainly a beautiful example of devotion to her Church and to those close to her, a Catholic Christian woman of loyalty and love. There will be no beatification for her, though I like to think of her as a saint in the Heaven she believed in. She will not hesitate to tell the angels to polish their shoes and halos, and her tongue may still have a somewhat bossy edge. But the heavenly host must have recognized pure goodness.

7 Kristallnacht in Fränkisch-Crumbach

The ninth of November was to be a fateful date for the Jews and non-Jews of Germany. In those days, however, news still travelled slowly to rural corners. Fränkisch-Crumbach did not realize the significance of the day. It was a backwater and they had to wait to hear what happened elsewhere. Across the country the synagogues were burning, shops owned by Jews were vandalized. Jewish men were arrested at random to be sent to the concentration camps of Dachau, Buchenwald and Sachsenhausen. Jewish children still left in state schools were expelled, as were any remaining university students. On the streets Jews were attacked. Some were killed.

Brother Ernst had rushed home from Mannheim, where he had witnessed the violence. We as children were not aware of lurking threats in Fränkisch-Crumbach, and went to bed as usual. We had avoided the horrors of 9 November and had an uneasy but uneventful 10 November, at least till night-time.

What was the ostensible reason for this outburst against us all? The answer lies in events that had taken place a few days before. The Nazis had hoped to orchestrate just such a demonstration to the fearful German Jewish community, and an occasion presented itself unexpectedly.

By the end of October 1938 all Jews of Polish origin living in Germany and Austria were rounded up and deported to Poland. Polish origin meant that they or their parents or grandparents had been born in Poland and had fled their homeland for fear of the pogroms periodically organized by both Polish locals and nationals, whose hatred of Jews was deeply rooted. Ironically, Jews had looked on Germany as a haven from Polish excess. Many of these so-called Poles had never been to Poland, could not speak Polish. That was of no interest to the Nazis. Birth in Germany was and still is no guarantee of citizenship. So Jews with even tenuous connections to Poland were pushed over the border, not allowed into the country proper by hostile Poles, unable to return for Nazi hatred. Some committed suicide, others were shot by German or Polish guards.

A 17-year-old Jewish boy, Herschel Grynszpan, who had fled to Paris from oppression in Germany and hoped his parents would join him there, had become desperate when he realized what had happened to them as Poles. His persistent enquiries at the German embassy for news of and help for his loved ones were ignored. He learnt quickly that the embassy was not likely to help his kind. In desperation he shot and wounded Ernst vom Rath, the third secretary at the embassy.

Germany was stunned: the Minister of Propaganda, Goebbels, led the world in manipulating modern media, the radio and the press. The wounded vom Rath's condition was constantly relayed to the nation. The press declared this attack to be part of a Jewish world conspiracy and threatened terrible reprisals. When vom Rath died on 9 November the Jewish community of Berlin issued a statement denouncing the assassination. It probably added fuel to the fire that was already kindled. That night, organized 'spontaneous' violence broke out everywhere. Storm troopers and others in uniform took part, but all who wished, and many did, were allowed to associate themselves with this show of indignation. If we as Jews were collectively responsible for the death of Jesus it was not difficult to believe that we were also all to blame for vom Rath's demise.

In Fränkisch-Crumbach the uneasy calm of 10 November was shattered for us late at night. I woke to thunderous knocking on the house door. Apparently it was not opened quickly enough, as I could hear the blows of an axe and wood crashing, then shouting and screaming. I do not know whether we, the children, screamed, but I was told 50 years later that poor, mentally disturbed Aunt Ida was beaten by the thugs and uttered unearthly shrieks. (It is thought-provoking that, with all else that has happened, this sound is still remembered in Fränkisch-Crumbach.) My sister Hannah came into my room. She had switched on the light but suddenly all was dark. We were terrified. Downstairs the voices were angry. We dared not approach, so we rushed to Uncle Gustav's bedroom. The poor lame man was struggling to heave his helpless body out of bed and to discover what caused the raging downstairs. The house had a back staircase leading down to an inner courtyard. Hannah and I fled downstairs, away from the tumult, barefoot in our nightdresses. It was a cold winter night. Father's car stood there. What else could we do? We jumped in and cowered together in the back. Then at the side of the house overlooking the courtyard we heard windows smashed. Someone was trying to attack the house from outside. The unexpected happened; a man whom we did not know came to the car. He did not speak to us – no comfort there – but he stood in front of the car and said he would deal with anyone who tried to approach or harm us.

I cannot say today how long we remained in our hiding place; it seemed like many hours of shivering with cold and panic. I know that I experienced there, at the age of nine, the greatest fear I have ever known. I have been in some dangerous situations since, not least during air raids over the north of England, but nothing to match the cold terror of that night. We did not know what had taken place in the house, where our parents were, whether we could ever go back, or what would happen to us if we did. Who would be there? In what state?

The night eventually came to an end. The vandals gradually tired and drifted away. The man who had installed himself as our protector vanished with them. We finally had the courage to steal back inside. The chaos we found stunned us. Poor Mother was standing in a daze, not knowing where to turn. She must have been desperate, but I was too young to understand. There were few answers to our questions. Father and Ernst had been taken away. Yes, she was sure they would be back soon. Was she? She did not tell us that they had been beaten up before they were seized. Nor did she tell us that our beloved, handicapped Uncle Gustav had been hurled down the stairs in the wonderful wheelchair he had designed himself. I wish he had died then but his martyrdom was not to end there. Aunt Ida's face was bruised; she was too distraught and sick to help.

Today I am still trying to piece together the aftermath, but find it difficult. I cannot remember how long it took to clear up the debris. Nor do I have any memories of helping, but I assume we all did. The windows and mirrors had been smashed, the pictures too. Every piece of furniture bore signs of the axe, though all was not totally destroyed. Curtains and bedding were ripped. The telephone had been torn out. The loss of the telephone was to prove prophetic: an order was soon proclaimed that Jews were allowed neither telephone nor radio.

I learnt afterwards what had upset Mother most deeply in all the destruction. Later, as a mother, cook and carer myself, I could understand her absolutely. Mother, like all the women in the village, preserved the food that we grew. There was much labour involved in doing so at the time: fruit and vegetables had to be picked, cleaned, peeled, graded, chopped. Some of it had to be cooked; jams had to be boiled; containers sterilized. The result was a splendid array of labelled glass jars, dozens of them, promising the family provisions for the winter. Now each jar lay smashed on the floor, the liquid mess oozing blood red through the heaps of broken glass.

I do not know when Mother heard that Father and Ernst had been taken to the concentration camp of Buchenwald after a night in the Fränkisch-Crumbach police cells. The name Buchenwald sounded innocent enough – 'Beech Wood'. As a child with a long German heritage, I knew what beech woods were and loved the mighty smooth grey tree trunks and the polished brown beech nuts, which we had early discovered to be inedible. Now, although only nine years old, I knew the name hid something sinister and cruel, and I was afraid. Buchenwald was not at that point a death camp, but many prisoners died there from beatings and torture, exposure and starvation. Even then I had heard of the cynical cards sent out to close relatives, that their loved ones had died of 'natural causes' and that they were to send money for the return of their ashes. Not that any of this was mentioned to us, the children, but information seemed to leak through, no doubt assisted by my efforts at eavesdropping. I was desperate to learn what I was not meant to know.

We never ventured outside the house now. I recall brother Ernst's return from Buchenwald. He had an American visa in his pocket, which may have provided him with a smattering of protection. At least here was a Jew who had got the message and whose presence would not be defiling the Fatherland for much longer. He had returned with shaven head and I had difficulty recognizing my normally well groomed eldest brother. He never spoke of his experiences in Buchenwald, not then and not later in the USA. He did tell us, however, that Father had encountered his brother Joseph there, who like so many others had been dragged from his home in Darmstadt. It was to be a foretaste of what the future had in store for them.

We seemed to wait a very long time for Father's release. In all, it was not more than a few weeks, but at the time weeks without news meant an eternity for a frightened family.

All Jews left in our village had gone through the same experience. We were not unique. Nor had the other villages and little towns of the Odenwald been spared. In Höchst, when Jewish property was attacked some families had escaped, like Herr Kahn's. Someone had secretly warned him to flee. Others had hidden in the nearby woods. The synagogue was destroyed with our little school. (I had no regrets about the school; it was a relief.) The synagogue of Michelstadt, an old and beautiful one, was vandalized on the inside only. Because of the neighbouring mediaeval timbered houses, express orders had gone out forbidding burning. In Reichelsheim the same destruction. Through eavesdropping, at which I had become expert, I heard that the prayer books and religious scrolls, venerated as sacred objects, had been burnt and that Jewish men had been forced to dance around the flaming pyre. The Reichelsheim cemetery – our nearest, where the Oppenheimers were buried – had been vandalized, the tombstones damaged and broken from their pediments.

Immediately after these events, German insurance firms announced that there could be no claims made on them for what had happened. The government decreed a fine on Jewish society as a whole, of one billion Reichsmarks. All damage visible to the German public caused by wrecking, looting and arson was to be repaired at once at the cost of the Jewish owners. Any remaining Jewish businesses were to be 'aryanized'.

Father finally came home before the winter was over. The occasion has lived with me through all the intervening years. The shame of my behaviour is still vividly with me. We must have heard he was coming. We waited, and when I knew he was due, I hid. Having overheard talk of concentration camps and their effect on the prisoners, I was frightened of what he would look and be like. The family called me and I did not come. Eventually I was found and I approached Father with great reluctance. I was longing to greet him with a smile but remained incapable. My fears were confirmed – he had changed. He was bruised, shrunk, ill and old. He seemed to be an invalid, and Mother spent much time nursing him.

What the village and Father's former employees felt about this I do not know. I do, however, remember a remarkable visit. Since 10 November a knock on the door had provoked panic, but here was a caller who surprised us. A servant appeared from the manor house with a basket sent by the baroness. There was beautiful bread and a bottle of wine for Father. Bread and wine. Had she been conscious of the symbolism behind her gift? Years later, when I thought of acknowledging this goodness, I was too late. She had died.

8 To the big city: Mannheim

A s a family, we had always been well known in Fränkisch-
Crumbach. Every inhabitant knew almost everyone else, but
the Oppenheimers had been prominent as the suppliers of the
first industry in the area, as good employers of a large workforce. My
father had had a political role to play and was one of the leaders of the
community. Since the pogrom unleashed on 10 November, we were not
only well known, we had become notorious. It was clear that continuing
to live there would not only be difficult, it would become impossible.
Jews living in villages throughout Germany became conscious of the
hostility around them and tried to leave for the nearest city. The great
advantage of rural life, knowing one's neighbours and feeling at ease
with them, no longer applied. It had become dangerous to be known
and recognized. Not that town folk were better disposed to Jews or less
hostile; they were indifferent to their neighbours and the many strangers
they encountered in their daily lives. They did not expect to know them
personally.

Mother still had links with the city of Mannheim. She had been born
there and some relatives remained. Our essential need was an income
and a home. Somehow she found work. She was appointed to direct and
manage the Jewish boys' orphanage in the city. Father would help, and
there would be room for their four remaining children.

It was at this time, just as the family was about to leave for Mannheim, that Feo and I contracted our whooping cough. My little sister and I were shattered to discover that we were to be left behind. It was explained to us that sick children could not be taken to a place where other youngsters might become infected with what was still a serious illness. It was devastating to contemplate the coming weeks alone in a house that was no longer safe. Young though we were, we realized that Uncle Gustav and Aunt Ida were not capable of looking after us. Mina, who seems to have kept an eye on us from afar, discovered our predicament and was determined to come to our rescue. She had never lacked courage, and this time again she defied the new Nazi laws and came to take charge of us. The household was gloomy. Aunt Ida was depressed and wretched. She often wept. Uncle Gustav too was morose. Our furniture and glass still bore the marks of destruction. Feo and I missed the others. We felt excluded.

But Mina fell sick. I soon realized that she was very ill. Although only nine years old, I knew that when a patient has difficulty speaking and breathing something serious must be amiss. Lame Uncle Gustav dragged himself to her bedside. We no longer had a telephone, and he told me that I must walk up the hill to call the doctor. I was shattered, petrified. To face the hostility of the outside world was too much to expect when I had not ventured through the door for many weeks. Since 10 November I had become a voluntary prisoner, and I refused to face the world outside. My longing for Mina's recovery was intense, but my fear and cowardice were greater. Uncle Gustav shouted at me. Mina was unable to speak. All to no avail. I hid. Finally I heard Uncle lumber downstairs and leave the house. In terror I peered through a window, certain that he would be attacked. There was this brave, lame old man, defiant in the middle of the road, heaving his incapacitated body between two crutches up the hill. No one approached him.

I have felt guilt and shame at various times in my life. Nothing could ever erase that moment of my greatest disgrace. The memory, even now, unsettles me.

Feo and I lived another few weeks with my aunt and uncle. Then we in our turn moved to Mannheim. I was not to see Uncle Gustav or Aunt Ida again. The official records said that both died in Theresienstadt. For long I was grateful that they had been spared the final hell of Auschwitz, that they were together, as they had been all their undemanding and infirm lives. However, a new *Gedenkbuch* ('memorial book') has now appeared on Theresienstadt, with the names, dates of arrival and departure (for the death camps or death itself), and places of deportation mentioned, it is clear that they had been separated. The sister arrived in Theresienstadt two months before the brother. Had he been allowed to take his crutches? Without them he could not move. There is an official form still to be seen in the archives at Worms. It was from the old people's home there, from which he was deported. Beside his name is the enigmatic phrase 'alleges he is unable to walk'. When I see the array of walking sticks, crutches and false limbs in museums in memory of the handicapped dead, I think of him and wonder. I cannot discard the questions that leap into my mind. Did Ida ever hear of his arrival? Was she able to find him among the many thousands? Could she help and comfort him? He was only to live for three weeks. After six months, Aunt Ida was apparently deported to Auschwitz after all. In Fränkisch-Crumbach there was a rumour that a guard had beaten my aunt to death. Who can know the truth today? Many prisoners died through random, arbitrary brutality. Concentration camp guards were not selected for their human compassion. Because of her mental instability and in the vile living conditions, she may well have suffered a bout of hysteria. What simpler way to deal with this old unhappy woman than to kill her? Who can know today, except the murderer?

In earlier years I remember both my uncle and aunt as mainly happy people. Childless themselves, they were always glad to see us children; we were their indirect progeny. But I wish I could now recall the smiles on their faces. When I think of them I only see Uncle Gustav, grim-faced, as he dragged himself up the hill to fetch the doctor, and Aunt Ida in the deepest wretchedness.

Before our departure, Mina had recovered from her pneumonia and Feo and I had ceased whooping and coughing. We were used to living as members of a large family, but in the boys' orphanage we found a larger one still, and on the whole we appreciated it. There seemed less reason to be afraid. We ventured out occasionally and no one shouted insults at us or threw stones. They did not know who we were. It felt good to be undiscovered and ignored. The orphan boys were friendly, and seemed to get on well with Mother in charge. Younger than most of the orphans, I was still overawed by the thought of orphanhood, and wondered how they had been able come to terms with it.

In Mannheim the synagogue had been destroyed by fire, but there still remained a Jewish school that we were to attend. I did not relish the thought of the long walk there and, perhaps wisely, we did not leave the orphanage in a crowd. We had learnt that we must make ourselves as invisible as possible. At school with pupils who had, in spite of the Nazis, been able to attend regularly, I knew that I lagged much behind my new schoolmates. I was ready to believe that I was rather stupid. This was the third school in my nine-year-old life, and I concluded that education was overrated. I found friends there eventually, but was not amused when these sophisticated city children thought my country accent droll. Many of my new classmates did not survive their childhood. In less than two years, they, with the rest of Mannheim's Jews, were among the first to be deported from Germany, an attempt to make the city *judenrein* (cleansed of Jews). It was an early experiment to assess how a city's population would cope with the process of deporting a part of its population. They coped well.

I was fortunate; I was not to be deported, but shocked when my parents announced at the beginning of June 1939 that I was to be sent to England. England? My scanty schooling had taught me little. I knew there was no *Führer* there. My father had been a passionate philatelist in better days and had shown me the special two-headed coronation stamp of a serious-looking king, George VI, and a gently smiling queen, Elizabeth. Where was England? Much further away than Holland, Belgium or France, and across the sea too. A feeling of injustice mingled with my initial distress. It was not fair that I was to be the first of the younger Oppenheimers to leave. Of course I understood theoretically that I was to be sent away for my safety. I had experienced enough to know that life was not going to improve for us, that we were in real danger. The November night still loomed large in the memory. I was keen to leave Germany now, but not alone and not for England. I had become used to the idea that we might all go to Argentina to join Werner, or to the USA to be with Ernst, but I was adamant that I did not want a future in England. Why live in a hostel with other girls, refugees from Germany whom I did not know? Why should I depart before Hannah, who was three-and-a-half years older than I? Clearly my parents loved me less. In fact Hannah and Michael were still on the waiting list for Holland. We have reason to be grateful today that they were unable to enter that country.

Britain had been wary of admitting refugees from Germany. However, they were acceptable if they brought a good supply of capital or were prepared to do certain jobs that British people found menial. Women without dependants could immigrate with a domestic permit for household work only, the escape route for my aunt Liese and my mother's cousin Lotte (Oppenheim). Scrubbing floors was preferable to an unknown but fearful future in their home country. The British government, however, was not enthusiastic. Foreigners were given to exaggeration, after all, and Jewish persecution in Germany, however abhorrent, was a strictly internal matter. Prime Minister Chamberlain was not about to offend Hitler. He had hoped to appease the *Führer* sufficiently in Munich to avoid a war. Antisemitism was not unknown in British society, though perhaps more subtle than in other parts of Europe or America.

There were, however, many good English people who did not agree with Chamberlain's policy. They wanted to help, and made their feelings known. Not only did English Jewish groups organize themselves into rescue and relief committees, there were also various church groups that did likewise, and there was the Society of Friends.

Quakers have always been in the forefront of helping those in need, especially the imprisoned and the persecuted. They were few in number, but the good they did was in inverse proportion to their size. There had been Quakers working in Germany since the end of World War I. The American and British Friends Service Committees had gone to help the starving, defeated Germans. They had set up offices in the larger cities, Berlin, Frankfurt, Nuremberg and Vienna. Over the years they grew aware of the rise of antisemitism and became deeply concerned. These Quaker centres started to help Jews to leave Germany. By 1938 it had become a massive operation both in the German Quaker offices and at Friends House in London.

In October 1938, Bertha Bracey, an English Quaker who had already given much help in Germany, headed the International Christian

Committee for German Refugees, set up in Bloomsbury, London, and known for evermore to all refugees as Bloomsbury House. After Kristallnacht, Bracey sent six Friends to various parts of Germany to assess the situation. They came back with unambiguous reports of danger, fear and suicides. Two Friends, Bracey and Ben Greene, accompanied Lord Samuel to see the Home Secretary to urge him to allow Jewish children a temporary refuge in England. That same evening, in a civilized and humanitarian gesture, Parliament passed an act providing for 10,000 children's entry permits. The plan was to be known as the *Kindertransport* scheme. At the beginning of December 1938 the first group of 200 unaccompanied children arrived in England. Bracey spent a long life doing good (she died aged 96 in 1989), but apparently the work that had given her most satisfaction was the rescue of us, the *Kinder*.

Of course, there were conditions set for our entry into Britain. A guarantee had to be furnished for each individual child, so that we should not become a burden to the state. Some of us had private sponsors, others were found guarantors through Bloomsbury House. Our parents were told that they had to try and fetch us as soon as possible and emigrate elsewhere (nothing would have pleased them more). Our stay was to be transitory. We were not to take up employment in Britain.

There was decency and humanity in a government that could act so speedily and permit us to immigrate without the customary papers and official red tape. Of the 10,000 children envisaged, 9354 made their journey to freedom from Germany, Austria and Czechoslovakia before war broke out in September 1939. The number saved was only a tiny fraction of those destined for murder. One-and-a-half million children eventually died. I honour Britain for this unparalleled gesture of goodness at a time when other countries turned a cold shoulder.

9   The *Kindertransport*

They gave me little warning, less than a week. By then I lacked the courage to resist. I was exhausted by the speed of events, the positive encouragement, the packing. What little time I had on my own I spent looking despairingly into the vacant, unknown future, hoping above all that this banishment would be short.

The night before my departure both my parents gave me a blessing. That is, they laid their hands on my head and said a prayer commending me to God's care:

> The Lord bless you and keep you;
> The Lord look kindly upon you and be gracious unto you;
> The Lord bestow favour upon you and give you peace.

This Jewish prayer is not unfamiliar to Christians. There was little else my mother and father could do. I can imagine their thoughts and their emotions.

My particular *Kindertransport* was to leave from Frankfurt. The transports went from the larger cities only. Parents were not allowed to take their children to the departing train. It would have been unseemly for the onlookers to witness 200 children and 400 parents trying not to weep and failing. But as we were a mere handful of children leaving Mannheim, our parents were at least able to accompany us to that station.

I did not know the other children. Mother asked the big boy in the departing group, a semi-adult of 13 or so, to look after me. I saw by his long face that a pathetic little strange girl, of all unnecessary burdens in his care, was the last thing he needed at that time. Our acquaintance was mercifully short, an hour or so. The goodbyes were not tearful, Mother insisted that we would soon be reunited, and I waved to them until I could no longer see them. I did wonder whether this was the last time, and tried to chase the thought away.

I remember little of the journey. My future companions, who had all travelled the same route, seem to remember it better. Re-reading that first letter I wrote home, I dutifully described that we had passed along the Rhine, and how, on crossing the border into Holland, we were given juice to drink by kind Dutch ladies. It must have been so, but I remember nothing except embarking at the Hook of Holland in the dark, hearing voices I could not understand. So that was English. Impossible to distinguish a single word. My worst fears were confirmed. I had been abandoned. The language I heard was barbarous. Someone took the trouble to speak to me, but incomprehension was to be my undoing. I wept. It did not matter. I knew no one and had no need to feel ashamed of crying. The kind incomprehensible person picked me up and carried me to a cabin.

No doubt I was totally exhausted, as I remember nothing till disembarkation at Harwich, where I arrived on 7 June 1939 with two suitcases and a *Kinderausweis* (child's ID). This bore my three original names, my enforced additional one, 'Sara', and in case of any doubt, a large 'J'. I was number 6295.

I was confused. One of my suitcases was with me, the other larger one had vanished. Suddenly I saw it standing on a platform, looking as forlorn as I felt. I made my lonely way to pick it up, and joined the other children in the train to Liverpool Street Station, London. Even before the bombardment, that station must have been the gloomiest of all. Or was it my misery that made Liverpool Street look dirtily dreary, grey and unwelcoming?

We were taken to a large hall, where we had to wait to be collected or dispatched, a group of tired, frightened children, each with a label hanging from the neck. Names were slowly called out, and children greeted relatives happily or strangers warily. I watched with interest, but my well-developed pessimism told me that there would be no one to fetch me and I would be left there to the end and beyond. My name was called out. Mrs Jacobson had not forgotten, and I was out of the hall before it was even half empty. I was relieved to find that Anna Jacobson spoke German. Mother had befriended her and her sister Rosi when they lived in Germany before World War I, the haven to which they had fled from the pogroms of Czarist Russia. This was our first meeting.

As we left, she was kind and calm in the midst of what I thought overwhelming traffic. The tall red omnibuses astounded me. Not knowing the expression double-decker, I described them as 'two-storied' in my first letter home. In Fränkisch-Crumbach the principal transport was still the horse and cart. There were only a few cars in the village and the nearest tarred road was two kilometres away. I had of course seen something of Frankfurt and Mannheim, but London was in a category of its own. Anna Jacobson told me years later that I was unwilling to enter the bus, expecting Jews not to be admitted.

A postcard was waiting for me from my parents; they had thoughtfully sent it ahead. I spent just three days with these kind friends in their small apartment in Eton Place, Chalk Farm, London. It was not possible to stay there indefinitely; they had made it their business to help people escape from Germany. They did this with energy and conviction and a minimum of fuss.

During that short time, their cleaning lady appeared to pity me and offered to take me to the nearby London Zoo. I was not keen to go but was too polite and too frightened to object. Only as I grew up did I realize why I did not enjoy zoos. They seemed so much like prisons. My companion was particularly keen to visit the special reptile house. My only knowledge of snakes, as a grossly under-educated ten-year-old, came from my reading. I had learnt that snakes were evil and cunning and I was terrified that I might disgrace myself by screaming, but I did not. Almost as disturbing as the snakes was the endless, incomprehensible chatter of the good lady; she was utterly well-meaning, but I was confused and upset and unable to convey my sense of bewilderment.

Leaving the Jacobsons was hard, but I knew I could not make my home with them. I was bound for a refugee hostel in northern England.

A short journey by the exciting London underground 'tube' brought me to Kings Cross Station to meet an English lady who was to accompany another ten-year-old, Stella Szipper, just arrived from Vienna, and myself to our final destination in the north. Our well-meaning companion showed us the mighty engine of the splendid train, the *Flying Scotsman*, that was to take us to Newcastle-upon-Tyne. It was difficult to be enthusiastic about a train into the unknown. Stella was visibly unhappy, she did not wish to talk, and our English custodian found communication difficult.

From Newcastle we finished the last lap of the journey by car, and I had my first ever view of the sea as we sped towards the coast at Tynemouth. At the Hook of Holland it had been too dark to see the sea, and at the port of Harwich I had either not noticed or we had been in some inner harbour. At Tynemouth, the sea was obvious and huge, infinite and relentless. I viewed it with fear. Continental Europe lay on the far side of that North Sea. If Britain had not been an island it would have been possible to walk back to Germany if I were really desperate. No matter how long such a trek might be, it was feasible. From Tynemouth, however great my longing, I knew that the land on the far side was beyond my reach.

We arrived at the hostel to a kindly welcome from the two matrons, Mrs Urbach and Mrs Sieber. They too had managed to enter Britain as domestics. When they arrived in this alien land, Mrs Urbach found a job as a cook with a London family, while her friend Mrs Sieber was employed as third parlour maid to a well-known aristocratic family who treated her badly. English households of the period were only too pleased to have domestic help who could be paid minimum wages, less than the local help might accept. They knew little about the plight of these desperate women forced to seek such work, and were not particularly friendly to Jews in any case.

It was not long before Mrs Urbach saw an advertisement for matron and assistant matron to a girls' refugee hostel in the north of England for girls who had left Germany, Austria and Czechoslovakia with the *Kindertransports* (jobs which could be had with a 'domestic permit'). Mrs Urbach persuaded Mrs Sieber, whom she had known in Vienna, to apply with her, and they were accepted by the Newcastle committee. Although their new work was arduous and demanded responsibility, it was less demeaning than the labour most other refugee women were forced to do. It was clear that the cleaning chores, the washing of laundry and dishes, the preparing of vegetables, could be done by the child inmates.

The ladies were middle-aged and firmly built, their figures well corseted, as was still the fashion in continental Europe and for the older female generation in Britain. Their solid persons must have inspired confidence. Mrs Urbach always wore a white overall or apron, had short white hair slicked back over the head, without a parting. Businesslike. She moved briskly, in spite of her weight, her small steps reverberating through the house. Mrs Urbach was practical, with feet firmly on the ground. Difficult to imagine her dancing.

Mrs Sieber, on the other hand, occasionally danced a few complicated steps to let us know that she had learnt and practised the art. She was self-consciously elegant, with a languid air. Her dark hair lay elaborately waved around her face, and her dresses fitted closely, with the skirt cut on the bias, so that it flared slightly, in the style of the twenties. Her shoes fastened with a strap, in keeping with the same fashion. No doubt her success as a woman dated from that period, and she had preserved her style. We were given to understand that she had been an admired beauty in her day, which seemed totally believable, and we looked at her with awe and wonder. Quite unlike Mrs Urbach, she conveyed an air of mystery that we would have liked to fathom.

I realized later that each one represented the accepted image of her personal profession: Mrs Urbach the director of a prestigious cookery school in Vienna, Mrs Sieber the owner and manageress of cinemas in the same city. Like us, the Jewish matrons had left as refugees; they were on their own, both widowed. They each had two sons, and fortunately for their peace of mind Mrs Urbach's sons were in the USA and both of Mrs Sieber's had found safety in England. The ladies' professions had ensured them independent means in their previous lives. We were fortunate that Mrs Urbach had directed the premier cookery school of Vienna, a city that was at that time famous for its cuisine. She had written a cookery book, with the proud title *So Kocht man in Wien* (*How We Cook in Vienna*), a bestseller.

Mrs Sieber's close contact with cinemas was an indirect advantage to us also. We were allowed, even encouraged, to visit the cinema, and delighted to do so, as in Germany Jews had been prohibited from all places of entertainment. It was of course a case of saving up pocket money. The allowance for my age group was a weekly 2d (2 old pence). This sum rose to its maximum of 3d by the end of the war.

After the *Anschluss* Austria had enthusiastically followed Germany in all anti-Jewish matters. Germany had burnt books by Jewish, foreign and anti-Nazi authors as early as 1933 and then banned any that had escaped the fire, whatever their subject. Mrs Urbach's cookery book should have been banned in Austria. It was, however, in such demand that the book had to be published, and the problem of an unacceptable Jewish author's name was solved by substituting another, this one more respectably 'Aryan' and male. Even after the war and the Holocaust, it was republished but still without Mrs Urbach's, the real author's, name. Not long ago, an Austrian friend in Britain recommended the book to me, under its false name. Publication has now ceased, not for reasons of honour, I imagine, but because its rich recipes are no longer fashionable in a cholesterol-conscious age.

Arriving at the hostel, I felt unnerved by the many pairs of eyes trained on us newcomers from a distance. We were being measured up. Would I be found wanting? Would they laugh at my country accent too as the Mannheim city girls had done? It was a relief to know that all but one spoke German.

There were at the time about 20 girls in the hostel. They came mainly from Germany, a handful from Austria and fewer still from Czechoslovakia. They seemed friendly enough to the newcomers, who felt very strange and afraid. The Austrian and German girls had all had similar experiences, though of course for us from Germany the awareness of antisemitism was almost lifelong.

As children we certainly benefited from Mrs Urbach's cooking. She astonished us at times by her culinary art, and for the girls from Germany, where food had not been plentiful and where much appeared in the guise of *Ersatz* (substitutes), her creations had a touch of magic. She was inventive, and her knowledge of food was extensive. During the war years, as food was rationed and became scarce, we children had no extras, no loving relatives in the country who grew vegetables or kept poultry, but we were well fed, sometimes with produce that others did not know about or would not have used. I remember elderberry flower fritters. She introduced us to Swiss *müsli*, unknown in England till long after the war, which she made of rolled oats (unrationed) and the wild crab apples and blackberries that we children were sent out to pick. As rationing became more severe, she displayed remarkable skill in adapting and supplementing. If we were lucky, rationing allowed us one egg per week. We never had a whole egg each, but Mrs Urbach knew how to scramble and add and stretch, so that the weekly egg per person might provide three different suppers for us all. Our physical well-being was assured.

The hostel had been created by a caring Jewish committee in Newcastle, conscious of Nazi persecution and wanting to help in a positive way. Once the *Kindertransports* were established it was discovered that there would be children for whom private homes could not be found. They decided to set up a home for girls. They thought and hoped that the duration of such a home would be limited, six months perhaps, or even a year; that our parents would make every effort to come and collect us as soon as possible to a life of freedom away from Germany, Austria and Czechoslovakia. This was of course our parents' dearest wish. The committee would thus have done a service of goodwill and charity that required time, effort and financial resources. They were to be heavily burdened. The war came all too soon. There we were, the refugee children, now unlikely to be gathered up by our parents in a foreseeable future. There they were, the Newcastle providers, having to face the fact that they were saddled with us for the 'duration' (this became a favourite wartime word, meaning unlimited time ahead). The hostel made heavy demands on their combined resources. The Jewish community was not large, and not all its members were in prosperous circumstances. They were to look after us for a long and unexpected seven years, providing a house, food, clothing, care and all the expenses, however modest, that the raising of 24 girls entailed.

I owe this community a tribute I have never paid. As a child I took it for granted that I might live, and expected to do so unquestioningly. I was wrong. In retrospect I thank the Jewish community of Newcastle and honour in particular the memory of the Summerfields, the Freedmans, the Wilkeses and the Collinses, who did so much to make life possible for us.

10 Tynemouth

Gradually I came to know the other girls. We had no inkling (nor would we have willingly accepted the idea) that we were to remain together for seven endless years. Inevitably we learnt to live as sisters, with occasional sisterly disputes and misunderstandings but also with a sense of sibling solidarity. We quarrelled only infrequently; we were good girls, understanding that we had to be, for our parents' sake, for the matrons' expectations, and for our own well-being.

After the first year we naturally split up into three groups of 'big ones', 'middle ones' and 'little ones', and were known by those group names. We knew exactly where we belonged in the hostel hierarchy. The distinctive grouping was to continue during the rest of our hostel lives, even when most of the big ones had left and we, the middle ones, had reached seniority. I was and remained in the middle group, the younger half of it, with Sophie Goldschmidt from Langensellbold, Germany, Elfi Reinert and Lisl Scherzer from Vienna. From Sophie to Lisl there was a range of a year and a half, six months separating each of us from the other. We became the closest of friends, almost sisters. Three of us from this group by chance remained in England, but Lisl, the youngest, left for Israel after the war.

I had arrived in June 1939 and was by no means the last girl to be taken in. New girls continued to appear. We seemed to welcome them as

59

friends. We knew what it felt like to be new and far from home. Paula Katz, a new arrival from Berlin, astonished me. She was all of 13, hence a grown-up girl compared with myself. She had long, pretty, wavy light-brown hair, which was loose about her shoulders. Her large eyes were sad as she sat on her bed in the dormitory, and I noticed that she had painted fingernails. I did not actually know the words 'loose woman' but that was my image of her. Very impressive. In Fränkisch-Crumbach I had not come across make-up, and I am sure my mother was innocent of it. She probably had little interest but surely less time. Paula's hair was soon tied back and out of the way. She looked less glamorous in time but no less sad. She remained an unhappy girl for as long as I remember her, and seemed to have no close friendship with the older girls.

Marion Mendelssohn too came from Berlin. Also 13, a tall, thin girl with a pale face and masses of dark curly hair. She was apparently con-nected across the generations to the composer's family. She too was sad and lonely in spite of the constant company that we had around us. Withdrawn, staring into space at times, she was slow in communicating with any of us. Witnessing sadness was normal for us, and we did not question. Years later, in an anthology on the emigration of children, Marion wrote that she resented her parents' telling of half-truths, not explaining fully the dangers that threatened them. She had convinced herself that her departure for England was parental rejection of a daughter no longer wanted.*

Of the big girls, some soon found their rightful place in the natural hierarchy. Eva was respected as the eldest and had a certain seriousness in looking after the younger ones. She had a sardonic tongue, thought of herself as a typical Berlinerin, and often made us laugh, which no doubt helped the healing process.

Annie Heufeld from Swabia was always ready to use kind and loving words to the younger children. There was much to learn. I had not darned stockings in my earlier life, nor washed my clothes. Annie showed us how. She had been taught to sew at home and was later kept busy at the sewing machine, turning old clothes into wearable garments, lengthening and

---

* Marion Karpf in Dorit Bader Whiteman, *The Uprooted: Hitler's Legacy*, New York and London, Insight Books, Plenum Press, 1993, p. 128.

letting out seams as we inevitably grew. I marvel now at her maturity. She was at most four years older than I, a child by any standard, but she could comprehend and comfort us so well when we were in trouble. She was always approachable. Why was this adolescent so patient with us, the younger children? She felt the separation from her parents as keenly as the rest of us. She had compassion with the widest smile. As she smiled, her face radiated a warmth from under her shiny dark hair, a glow that I felt immensely comforting. She showed understanding beyond her years.

Among the middle ones, Sophie proved the most efficient and we envied her speed and capability in the despatch of tedious tasks. The rest of us sometimes irritated her, but she was basically good-natured and forgiving when we mocked her. We combined well as a quartet and felt a bond of friendship among all four. Lisl laughed often, was easily amused, and we older three were quite benevolent, making excuses for her, as she had not yet reached the important age of ten, a landmark Sophie, Elfi and I had already passed.

As middle ones we felt superior in our seniority to the little ones but we did look after them and occasionally played with them. We sometimes even cherished their sayings, as those of us with younger siblings had done at home. We all remember the youngest, Lea Roth, not normally willing to say much in her strange new surroundings, who when fruit was given out and she received only a little piece, was unexpectedly heard wailing, 'Ich will auch eine grosse, dicke Birne!' ('I also want a big fat pear!'). This became a sentence we were to use time after time ourselves; it became a kind of binding mantra among us.

Lea was the third of three Roth sisters who arrived together from Borken near the Dutch border. Hilde, the eldest, was the most serious, told by her parents at the age of seven to look after Frieda and Lea, the younger ones. She was ever conscious of her duty, and the three sisters spent much time in each other's company, three little shiny black-haired children, all with fringes over their foreheads, which seemed to hide their beautiful dark eyes and their little faces. For a long time they communicated only with one another in a little sisterly huddle.

For a short period a little boy joined this army of girls. I remember only his first name, Rolf, and his famous sentence, which has also echoed down the years. He too must have been as homesick as the rest of us, lonely as the only boy among so many girls. One evening at supper he cried. When asked why he was crying, and ill-prepared to put his real distress into words, he blurted out, 'Die Lore schüchtert mich ein!' ('Lore intimidates me!'). It cannot have helped him that we all laughed in spite of his misery, as Lore was the shyest, sweetest little six-year-old, and smiled but rarely spoke at this early time in the hostel.

Poor Lore Freitag, so young, separated like the rest of us for the first time from her parents, not surprisingly wet her bed, almost nightly. She was beaten daily by our protecting ladies. Small as she was, she had the task of washing her bedding in the morning. She could barely lift the heavy wet sheets out of the bath, in which we washed the larger pieces of laundry and then struggled to hang them out. I was an ignorant ten-year-old, but felt indignant on the little girl's behalf. I knew this could not be the right treatment. Had I by then heard of that other Viennese, Dr Sigmund Freud, whom I am sure our Viennese matrons knew, I would have been even more shocked. Later, many years later, I discovered that Lore's nocturnal problem worried her immediate friends, little girls like herself, who, sleeping on either side of her in the dormitory, thought to tie a piece of string from their own wrists to Lore's and would try to wake her at some point in the night so that she could go to the bathroom and avoid another bedwetting. It occasionally worked.

One of these little ones suffered more immediate distress than the rest of us. This was a little Czech girl, Daša. We all were genuinely fond of her. A guileless child who managed to smile broadly whenever she was not weeping. And she wept often. She was the only one in the house who could not speak German. Nor had she acquired any English. At the age of seven, she had arrived from Prague with the Reiss girls, who had looked after her and interpreted for her. It was a blow for Daša that Vera and Liesel Reiss left for Australia just before the outbreak of war. Their cousin Helga stayed. She spoke a little Czech but not enough to be really helpful to Daša. She remained a friend of Daša's but could be only a limited comfort. We all learnt important Czech phrases such as: 'Ne plac, Dašenka!' (Don't cry little Daša!). Because Daša felt so lost, she inevitably lost her property in her confused unhappiness. Her constant questions started with 'Kde muj...?' ('Where is my...?'). I still remember 'cepice' ('cap'), perennially lost. This was my only Czech, but it has survived.

Poor Daša. We were all conscious of our foreign names, which sounded strange to our schoolmates and sometimes caused them mirth. But Daša, who spoke not a word of German, had the added ironic misfortune to have 'Deutsch' as a family name!

Not long after my arrival, two more little ones came, sisters also, so different from the dark little Roths. The Adamecz girls from Breslau were the very picture of the 'Aryan' species so desired by the new regime, very blond and blue-eyed. The older one, another Ruth, aged seven, the younger, Inge, five. The two girls came from a mixed marriage, an 'Aryan' father and a Jewish mother. The father did what good Germans who had been misguided enough to marry a non-'Aryan' were asked to do. He left his wife and three little girls. Mrs Adamecz had bravely let her two little girls leave for the unknown, but kept the youngest, a toddler, with her. Inge and Ruth treasured the photo they had of little Gretel, a glorious cherub. We knew each other's photos intimately, we showed them so often. As time went on, these young sisters seemed to suffer more at the hands of the matrons than others in the hostel. They still remember it well. Like the Roth parents, Ruth's mother had put the burden of Inge's care on her seven-year-old shoulders. Ruth was never to forget her mother's parting words, and took this responsibility seriously for the rest of their combined childhood. Inge on the contrary was happily mischievous, full of fun, and left the anxieties to Ruth. The latter was often lost in thought, her face grave and unsmiling. She seemed to cope with her younger sister without any anger, more by example, while Inge smiled through her dimples, charmed and delighted all onlookers.

We all lived in the constant hope that our parents would manage their escape, would come to collect us and restore us to the cherished intimacy of our former family lives. The waiting was frustrating, but we were fairly confident it would happen. Our parents had promised this, and our wishes and prayers must carry some force, we felt. There was proof that it was possible. Some of the girls in the home were taken away: Lotte Jacobson from Hamburg left, as did Hannah and Lea Kohn from Leipzig. From Prague their parents gathered up Vera and Liesel Reiss en route to Australia just days before the outbreak of war. The departure of Lucy Pressburger, one of the most senior girls, saddened us. She was extremely popular as a kind and happy girl, and had already distinguished herself as a swimmer in her native Austria, where her talents were no longer required. She had promised to teach the younger children to swim, and this was not to be. Mostly our feelings were of envy. We were not surprised that we never heard from any of them again. They had gone to a better life. Perhaps we would not have acted differently.

Slowly I began to adapt to my new life in England. It seemed alien both outside and within the hostel. The German girls mocked my friend Elfi for using Austrian expressions, some of which were distinctly confusing, even when we spoke of ordinary objects. In German a cup is 'eine Tasse', where the Austrian word is 'Schale'. The word 'Tasse' exists in Austrian German but means a saucer, whereas saucer, in what I considered the more logical language, is 'Untertasse'. And I was laughed at not for my country dialect as I had expected, but for using German words that sounded strange to the Austrian ear. Although the Austrians were in the minority, they had right on their side. Both matrons were Austrian. In any linguistic dispute, they joined forces against 'the Germans'. Our German was the inferior language. We skated on thin ice here; our hatred of the Germans of Germany and for what they had done to us was intense. None of us any longer called them Nazis or Christians, as we had done when we were after all ourselves still Germans. They were now all Germans. So for those of us who had come to the hostel from Germany to be mocked for our 'German' accents and expressions, and to find ourselves tribally defending our brand of 'German' seemed bizarre even at the time.

Meanwhile Germany had declared us 'stateless'. They had taken away our German nationality. I knew what it felt like to be a German national and I was not comfortable with that feeling once the war broke out, but I failed to understand the meaning of 'stateless'. We had after all been born in a real place with its own nationhood, a genuine 'state'. Years later, when I first heard of weightlessness I imagined there was a similarity, but as I could not cope with the principles of physics, another neglected part of my sketchy education, both conditions remained a mystery to me. I tried to see myself in this stateless limbo, but could not.

Sometimes the anti-German feeling in the hostel spilled over. The Austrian matrons were not above describing certain behaviour as 'typically German'. It was the greatest insult, and deeply hurtful. It was made clear to us, the German majority, that the Austrian and Czech girls had more charm, more grace of manner and speech. They were more willing to smile. Even at the early age of ten, I realized the injustice of this viewpoint. Was I alone, I wondered, in understanding that to date the German girls had endured six years (a long time for a ten-year-old) of humiliating discrimination, whereas the Austrians had faced just over a year and the Czechs a mere few months? My sense of injustice was to get me into trouble often in the coming years. I was inclined to mutter and growl, 'That's not fair', words resented by adults in charge of children.

We learnt to live together, to become used to a community when we had previously lived in our smaller family units. It must have been particularly hard for the very little girls, some barely older than tots. We made friends, and we learnt to look after each other. The big ones naturally helped the little ones with washing and dressing. We washed each other's hair. We learnt to wash our own clothes, to darn socks and stockings, to keep our possessions tidy. We soon acquired duties in the house, preparing food in such ways as peeling potatoes and cleaning vegetables; laying fires and bringing in fuel; washing up and ironing; setting the tables for each meal. We did not complain about duties, and did them cheerfully on the whole.

We started in the local schools, the middle and little ones going to the Tynemouth junior school, the older girls below the age of 14 attended a secondary school at North Shields. Fourteen was the official school leaving age, and those older stayed in the hostel and helped to run the household.

In those few months before the war most of us received letters from our families. The mail was the exciting event of the day, and we all waited for it with longing. We ourselves wrote regularly. Looking at my letters now, I know they do not reflect my unhappiness at the time. I am surprised to see how often and insistently I write, 'It is very nice here'. But I also remember that all letters were inspected. We did not seal our own letters. Some girls were in trouble for what they had written. This censorship may have been to protect our parents from unnecessary worry, but it was more likely a general practice in the institutions of the day. Children cannot be trusted. They see reality as it is. Later, friends who had been at English boarding schools at the same time told me that their letters too were read by the teachers.

I wrote home about the food that we were served, but I was careful, perhaps even tactful. English breakfast cereal was a new idea to those of us who had been brought up on bread or rolls for that first meal of the day. I thought cornflakes a very unusual dish but quite delicious. Shredded wheat on the other hand appalled me. I was convinced it was straw for breakfast.

The German girls did not always enjoy Mrs Urbach's typically Austrian cuisine. It was simply a case of unfamiliarity. We discussed this amongst ourselves with much childish irreverence, deploring the use of smothering breadcrumbs on every dish and the sweet-sour Austrian flavourings, as well as some of the desserts, appropriately named *Mehlspeise* ('dish made with flour') in Austrian German. I refrained from writing about such trivialities. I did appreciate the fruit that appeared, not a by-product of Viennese cookery but one of the benefits of the British empire. Bananas and oranges had been a luxury in the Germany of the day, and grapefruit was a new exotic discovery.

My letters home are misspelt, poorly written and haphazard. My schooling at the age of ten had been sparse, amounting in all to less than two years, but I knew that letters represented a lifeline. Sometimes I was conscious of not wanting to worry my parents, at other times my anxiety comes through with questions such as, 'When are we going to Argentina? When are you coming?'

I added gratuitously and probably accusingly that so and so's parents had managed to come for her. I asked absurdly, 'When shall I send a birthday letter to brother Ernst when I don't know how long the letter will take?'

Greatly worried, I told them I was afraid that the Jacobsons might invite me to London and whatever should I do, as I would be far too frightened to travel on my own without the help of the English tongue. I seemed to remember to greet my friends who were left behind; I often asked after Uncle Gustav and Aunt Ida, and I almost always remembered to send love to Mina. I told them inconsequential things: I was wearing knee socks for the first time, or wanted to know who was sleeping in my bed at home. I tried not to worry them about my welfare but clearly was not as thoughtful as I should have been. In a letter sent a year after my leaving home I told them, in rather poor German, that I had now been gone one year and that so much had changed during that time that I felt I had been away for five.

As for the letters from our parents, they were read and re-read, clutched and treasured under the pillows and wept over. These were our only truly private possessions. We learned to share at an early age, and we were not ungenerous with others, but we did not share our letters from home. It was not only personal pet names that we were afraid of exposing, it was the sweet and loving expressions of comfort which would sound absurd when read by others, and of course such exposure might reduce us to tears in public, a circumstance to be avoided at all costs. Mother often addressed me as her dear 'Ruthkind'. I kept that a secret.

Letters from siblings were another matter. The fact that Hannah had arrived in England made a positive difference to my existence. We knew that we were unlikely to meet, but we corresponded. She had managed to leave Germany in August 1939 with the help of British Quakers, among the last to be able to do so before hostilities between Britain and Germany stopped all contact. She lived briefly with an elderly Quaker lady in London, Miss Storr. They liked each other but Hannah was soon sent to the Sussex coast. There was a policy at the time to evacuate as many children as possible from London, as war was imminent and immediate bombing was feared. I knew she was about as far from me as it was possible to be in the same country, but it was still good to know that there were now two of us in England. I was in the distant northeast and she in the deepest south. The hostel girls found it easier to speak of our siblings than of our parents, and I was prepared to read out snippets from Hannah's letters, which were usually humorous and optimistic. She never shared her worries.

Her letters home were cheerful. Quite as anxious as I about the family's welfare, she managed to couch her fears in less crude terms, avoiding worries for those left behind. She described her move from London to Worthing, Sussex, where she and two other girls were sent to live with an elderly lady on her own: 'We are with a very nice old lady, she is very proper and elegant, but that does not matter. I am behaving better than I have ever done before, you would be truly surprised if you could see me.'

Also, and this must have comforted our parents, 'I recently had a six-page letter from Ruth, which she wrote no doubt with much sighing, because I told her I did not want a letter from her that was less than eight pages long'.

She assured our parents that she was making good progress at school and in the English language, adding for good measure and credibility, 'Really', as an afterthought. She happily described the performance of a magician she had seen. She told an anecdote of someone teaching her to swim, but since she had discovered a large hole in the seat of her swimming costume, had spent the rest of the time by the sea sitting on the hole to conceal it.

Hannah turned 14 that same August. There would be no more schooling for her; she would now have to earn her living. Germany had deprived her of an education and she was unqualified. She was to be mature before her time.

11 Wailing siren on a quiet Sunday: war

Like almost everyone else I remember exactly where I stood as the siren wailed that Sunday morning, 3 September 1939, announcing hostilities between Britain and France, the Allies, and Germany, henceforth the enemy. Hitler had just invaded Poland. The radio with Prime Minister Chamberlain's broadcast had been turned up somewhere in the house, so that we might all hear. I could not understand very much, but managed to digest the word 'ultimatum'. This was what the newly allied countries had apparently given to Germany two days earlier. What was it? A package? A letter of some sort? It seems this 'ultimatum' had not been returned or had not been accepted by Hitler. So now there was to be a war.

In the hostel that day we were trying to celebrate my friend Lisl's tenth birthday. She was now my age, and we felt closer. The celebration was not uppermost in our minds. Lisl, a happy, cheerful girl, understood what was happening, as I did. We were in our large dormitory looking out towards the sea that separated us from home. Home was suddenly even farther away. As the sirens continued their eerie moaning, we wondered whether bombs would drop immediately. We had been told in school that the wailing of the siren would precede an air attack. I was confused about war; I had seen numerous pictures of battles, with soldiers on horseback swinging swords and sabres. I had also seen guns, cannons and tanks, not so long ago in Germany. We knew, too, of the French and German soldiers ready to face each other on the Siegfried and Maginot lines, and in the trenches.

In school we had been trained to go quickly and quietly to the underground air-raid shelter, a process that was quite fun and not too serious. We eventually learnt to put on gas masks, which we always had to carry to and from school. This too provoked uneasy giggles as the masks of tight new rubber were sticky and smelly and not easily fitted over the face. The stubby round air filter at the end of the mask had a pig-snout-like appearance. During practices we saw how monstrous and absurd we all looked. I do not think we were frightened of these extra signs of war, though I always peered somewhat anxiously at the pale paint covering the tops of the bright red pillar-boxes. This was a special compound designed to change colour in the event of a gas attack.

Even the youngest among us understood very quickly that contact with our parents would henceforth be more tenuous. One could no longer communicate directly with Germany. It was enemy territory, and to hear that the Germans were our enemies was hardly news.

The radio, or wireless as we called it then, took on a new importance. I understood how vital it was to learn English, though my progress in the language was very slow. The idea that our parents would come to collect us faded. We still hoped fervently that somehow they would manage to emigrate to the Americas, none of whose countries were involved in hostilities. The world that might still accept them, albeit reluctantly, had shrunk: Australia, Canada and South Africa, as well as other parts of the old British empire were now no longer open.

Almost overnight, the aspect of Tynemouth changed. Suddenly most of the seafront was no longer accessible. There was barbed wire along the beaches. We were told that the Germans might land here. Everyone had to put up blackout curtains. No chink of light must ever show in the dark. If enemy planes were to fly over, they must not be able to see habitation, industry or transport systems. Cars and buses had to have special shielded headlights, which beamed downwards only. The times of blackout were strictly announced and observed. Shop windows and large glass surfaces had tape criss-crossed over them to avoid their shattering into tiny fragments in the event of explosions. Men and women appeared in uniform, mostly of unbecoming khaki, relieved by Air Force blue or, even more attractive, the dark blue of the Navy.

As children we had learnt early not to speak about our personal anxieties, but we were all perplexed as to how we should contact our parents. Mostly they solved the problem for us. It was they who thought of friends and relatives in neutral countries to whom they could write, hoping that these would forward letters to us. All of us – except those girls whose parents, as 'Poles', had been expelled from Germany or Austria into a Poland that rejected them – had some contact with home.

In my case and my sister's (although she lived hundreds of miles away in Sussex), it was Hannah's school friend Doris Katz, a refugee from the Nazis in Holland, who faithfully sent on the mail. Doris came from the pretty little mediaeval town of Michelstadt in the Odenwald, which had had a small but long-settled Jewish community. It treated its Jews badly during Kristallnacht, and Doris must have thought herself fortunate to be in Holland. Aged barely 14, she acted responsibly in sending on our mail. She often enclosed not only a letter to Hannah but also tried to send encouraging notes to our parents when she forwarded our letters. She faithfully recorded to them what Hannah had said in personal letters to her, assuring them that we were well and added, 'Das ist die Hauptsache' ('that is the main thing').

By then, naturally, all mail was censored and some was lost, but Doris succeeded in getting most of it through. Unfortunately this communication ceased when the Germans overwhelmed Holland with a powerful and rapid invasion in May 1940. We were never to hear from Doris again. Together with other refugees from Germany, as well as Dutch Jews, she was to die in the death camp of Maidanek, Poland.

Our parents were desperate to stay in touch. One way was to use brother Ernest (he had acquired that extra 'e' in the USA) as an intermediary, but it took many weeks to send letters across the Atlantic and back when they were only meant to cross the North Sea. Mother was resourceful. She had always kept in touch with a friend from her early teaching days in Kaunas, Lithuania. This was Erna Fischel. Lithuania was not yet in Hitler's path and had remained neutral. Post from home started to reach us via Kaunas. Erna was so good and meticulous. Not only did she send everything on, she translated Mother's letters for the benefit of the English censor, hoping thus to avoid too long a delay. Her English was remarkably good. She always found time to write a warm little personal note to accompany a letter from home, calling me 'dearie' and letting me feel her concern. I do not suppose that she had ever managed to travel as far afield as Britain. She was a busy woman, teaching all day and coping with her elderly invalid mother the rest of the time. I know that she always wrote to my mother when she sent on our letters, and must have done her utmost to reassure her.

This scheme too collapsed when the German armies turned east towards the Soviet Union. Lithuania was overrun very quickly. The country once had a very large Jewish population which was almost completely wiped out in the war. From the day the Germans invaded their country, Lithuanians could murder Jews for sport, and they did. Today it matters little whether Germans or Lithuanians exterminated Erna and her mother, old Mrs Fischel. No exact information is available. Death certificates are not issued in mass slaughter.

For many of us, communication with our loved ones ceased when most of Europe was under German control. There was much to worry about, particularly after the defeat of France and the debacle of Dunkirk. Victory for the Germans looked all too likely that summer. We, the refugee children, grasped the reality of our situation: defeat for Britain would be an even greater disaster for us. No one will ever understand why Hitler did not persist with his invasion of England and turned against the USSR instead. It was to be his undoing, though we did not know it then. It was to be our salvation.

12 The matrons of Vienna and their charges

During that first year of the war even the younger ones among us understood that life would be very different, that our future was uncertain, that we must hope for peace. We knew that there could be no peace for us without a German defeat.

We were all in the hostel for the same reason: we were refugees from a homeland that had become too dangerous for us. But this did not mean that we always felt united. Our matrons were not experienced in the raising of children. They had sons, and we were all girls. As professional women they had enjoyed considerable domestic help and child care, and were not familiar with the daily problems and the strain of bringing up other people's children. Nor can we have been easy. The little ones were openly homesick; our youngest had arrived aged three. The rest of us managed to conceal our feelings most of the time. Although we were conventionally good girls, we were unhappy girls, and to make matters worse, most of us were or became adolescents.

There were four girls in the hostel whom we considered particularly fortunate. They each had one parent apiece in England. Ilse Gross (from Vienna) and Edith Rossmann (from Düsseldorf) had mothers, Helga Reiss (Vienna/Prague) and Lisl Scherzer (Vienna) each had a father. Did they know how we envied them? I do not think so. They seemed in fact less anxious and more contented than the rest of us, and showed signs of greater confidence. They were perhaps treated better by the matrons because of the existence if not the constant presence of the parents. The rest of us were not unaware of this. Helga's father actually lived nearby, once we had moved to Windermere. He had found work as cook in a hotel up the road. The poor man did not know how to cook, but Mrs Urbach advised him and he learnt. The mothers tried to find domestic work locally, and managed for a time at least. Lisl's father had joined the Pioneer Corps, the lowest form of military life in wartime Britain and the only available work for most male enemy aliens. He visited her regularly when he had military leave and she was generous with him. We were allowed to share her father, an extraordinarily kind man who did not object when we intruded and allowed him little time alone with his daughter. If he brought sweet goodies, they were shared. He, she and we (the middle ones, Sophie, Elfi and I) took that for granted. He played and joked with us and understood our needs. I do not remember him without a smile, though he too must have been anxious about his wife left behind alone in Vienna. He was a reassuring presence, our father figure.

The standards of behaviour we were expected to aspire to were in the best nineteenth-century tradition. Vienna, whose days of glory were in the past, had in some aspects not advanced very far into the twentieth century. We were not allowed to shout, or to laugh loudly. This was unseemly. A pity, as we so rarely felt like laughing. Rules were established, and although I expected this I thought some rules very silly. That was arrogant of a ten-year-old. We were not allowed to run up the stairs, it was unladylike. In my German home we had taken it for granted that we ran up the stairs and slid down the very appropriate broad banisters. For a country child from primitive Fränkisch-Crumbach, I was unaware of social aspirations. Becoming a lady was not one. There were certain ways to hold a fork, there was a special art to tilting one's soup plate, to cutting one's bread, activities that had never caused me any problems in the past.

The Austrian girls clearly were more ladylike than the others. I took certain Austrian expressions very literally. I liked 'Grüss Gott' as a friendly greeting, but as one who liked words to be exact was obliged to draw the line at 'Küss die Hand, gnädige Frau', which did not mean what it said, 'Let me kiss your hand, gracious lady', but merely 'good day' without any accompanying action. This slightly unreal behaviour astonished me, and even allowed me an occasional suppressed giggle.

Speaking the enemy language was a dilemma. I am sure it was right that we should make every effort to speak English, but to prohibit German, as the matrons did at times, was absurd. Some of us had nothing else. So we had to remain silent. Adolescent girls were not likely to comply with that rule, and we started whispering to each other in German. That was very rude, we were told: only vulgar people or dishonest folk whispered. Whispering was forbidden. I did understand that the special attention paid to artificial good manners was meant for our own good. We had to make our way in a new life and to impress and charm, but I also knew that this was not my way.

My greatest longing was to read. As children at home, we had derived pleasure and comfort from books. I also knew that the magic of books could let me escape, however briefly, from my immediate surroundings. We had not brought any German books. In the little luggage we managed to carry there was no room. It was the greatest deprivation. The excitement, relaxation and above all consolation that comes from reading were denied. The house, perhaps rightly, had no German books. We were after all in a country whose language we should learn as quickly as possible. A kind donor had given the hostel a whole row of English volumes for the young. I looked at them eagerly and tried to read, pronouncing each word to myself phonetically, realizing that I was not making an English noise, but worse, I understood nothing. It was frustrating to the point of tears.

Not long after my arrival I was sent shopping, my first outing by myself to the grocery, my first time alone in a totally English environment with no one to help me. I had not yet had the courage to try any English on my own and I was afraid. I knew enough about life in the hostel to understand that I had no right to refuse, no right to say I was too frightened, and I departed miserably to buy a half pound of almonds. I had been given the English word, which the matron rightly knew I did not have. She had even spelled it for me, which intrigued me for I was intelligent enough to see immediately that 'almond' in English and 'Mandel' in German was almost an anagram. But even if I had remembered the word I know I could not have pronounced it correctly in English. Where was the 'l'? Germans did not ignore letters that were part of a word. It was illogical. I had to return and confess that I had forgotten the word. This time they wrote it down for me, but not without telling me that I was a stupid child.

We muddled through. Because we lived with learners of English we did not master the language as correctly or as quickly as did other child refugees who had been taken in by English families. We eventually spoke 'Immigranto', a German-English mixture, and before the end of the war German was cast aside and we spoke only English. On the whole most of us retained some kind of foreign accent, which irked us, but we were unable to change it.

For Daša, the language problem was greater than for the rest of us. Her native tongue was a Slav language, whereas German is an ancestor of English and we German speakers were able to recognize the links and common vocabulary, thus learning more quickly. Daša was to have a very erratic history. In London, the Czech government in exile (Czechs were 'friendly' aliens) had certain powers and was supported by the British government. It decreed that all Czech refugee children in the country were to be sent to a new Czech boarding school to be set up in Wales. The goal was to preserve their language and culture and bring up citizens who could return to Czechoslovakia when the war was over, as Czech citizens, not as strangers. By the time the school was ready, our friend Daša, not having had any opportunity to speak Czech with the rest of us, had forgotten much of her mother tongue; she had acquired indifferent English and German. At her new school she was once more in a language predicament. Moreover, she knew no one, she was again alone. The school eventually closed and Daša was sent to another hostel. We were unable to forget her.

We called both ladies 'Frau Doktor', a courtesy title acquired through marriage to men with doctorates. The term implied a certain level of wisdom, which in so many ways our matrons lacked.

At some point in our first year there was an outbreak of head lice in the school. Immediate hysteria. We had to comb our hair daily with a toothcomb. It was decided that girls with curly hair were to have it shorn. I am not sure that head lice care whether they reside in straight or curly hair. My opinion was not asked before I had to submit to a boy's haircut. So did Marion Mendelssohn, Helga Reiss and the very blond sisters Inge and Ruth Adamecz. Inge, at six, screamed through the shearing. She was a pretty child and knew that her loss of curls would not enhance her image. The rest of us hardly acquiesced. We suffered this indignity with set jaws and a sense of injustice. Although we were all unhappy at this drastic change in our appearance, we had by then learnt that we must accept such treatment from our elders in silence. On one or two hostel photos there are signs of sullen expressions under the reduced coiffure; on another, little Ruth Adamecz has put her hand over her face. I saw little relevance or consolation on being told that this cut was fashionable, and known as the 'Eton crop'. I did not care who or what Eton was and I intensely resented any kind of crop.

Of course that was a minor misery. Inge and Ruth had more to suffer than a hair cut. They were frequently accused of lying and stealing (taking a biscuit from a plate when no one was looking was a major theft), and locked up for a long time in a dark cupboard under the stairs. Ruth recalls with great bitterness that aged eight she once took a bar of chocolate and shared it with the younger children. Helga, who was the most fortunate among us, as she had a father less than a mile away in Windermere and a mother safe in the USA, having eaten her illegal share, told her father, who then took a photo of Ruth, getting her to hold a stone to her mouth, perhaps in place of the missing chocolate, and wrote over the ensuing photo, 'THIEF'. The photo was then shown to everyone. People had scant knowledge of psychology then, but was such cruelty necessary for a child who was always and obviously deeply unhappy?

We had visitors to the hostel. The Newcastle committee that financed the hostel and was the ultimate arbiter of our fate took its duties seriously, and occasionally different members of that committee came to help, guide and encourage the matrons in what was a difficult task. When they came, the girls were expected to appear, clean and tidy, as a group in the living room. It was our duty to smile and look agreeable. (If one of us did not smile, she was rebuked later.) Eva Less, with her sharp Berlin sense of humour, cynically called this the *Affenschau* ('monkey parade'), and the name stuck. I hated this inspection but felt somewhat better about the absurd performance when I thought of the monkey business.

The hostel matrons did not have an easy time. The first winter of the war, 1939–40, was hard, with unexpectedly low temperatures. Britain has a temperate climate, but every now and then there is a severe cold patch. On the whole English houses were not built to withstand unusual frost. The heating was not as efficient as continental European or American systems, and water pipes froze and burst. It was possible that no one knew they had to be lagged. This happened at the Tynemouth hostel. Suddenly, in the first February of the war, we found ourselves without heating or water. Mrs Urbach and Mrs Sieber worked hard with all of us to try and clear up the damaging floods from burst pipes, but it was obvious that we could not remain in the house. The committee, ever helpful, rapidly organized temporary accommodation for the children in family homes in Newcastle and Whitley Bay, a little coastal town further north.

My friend Sophie and I were sent to a couple with a baby in Whitley Bay. Although we had been in England just over half a year, our English was neither good nor fluent. Our hosts showed little sympathy for us. We were young children but sensitive enough to understand fairly quickly that we were unwelcome guests. We tried to keep as invisible as possible, but this was not easy. We had been given a pleasant enough bedroom with a double bed. Neither of us had ever shared a bed, but discovered the advantage of this, as the cold of the unheated room was intense in that exceptional winter. We stayed some hours in the bedroom during the day but eventually had to come downstairs, as we were too cold. Mr and Mrs Potash barely spoke to us, though we shared meals with the family. One day after lunch, not wanting us around, Mr Potash threw some coins across the table and told us to go to the cinema. Sophie and I were wretched. I do not remember which of us, as we left the house, proposed that we should return to Tynemouth, but this was what we decided to do. We had scant knowledge about north and south, but I knew that we must make for the sea, face it and turn right. This we did, leaving our few possessions in the home of our reluctant hosts. I cannot remember how many miles there are between the two towns, but it seemed a long trek for two young girls, Sophie nearly 12 and I a month short of my eleventh birthday. A very cold trudge in a northern February. Some of the way we were able to walk along the sands, which we preferred, some of the way we had to follow the coast road.

It is to the credit of Mrs Urbach and Mrs Sieber that in spite of their astonishment at our return they did not scold us – we had feared this – but allowed us to stay. It was probably my best time in the hostel. In spite of the spartan conditions in a waterless, cold house we enjoyed more of a family atmosphere in that hard late winter than I was to experience at any other time in my long years there.

To mention our aching longing for home was an unspoken taboo. That was far too dangerous a subject, too close to the unbearable. We did talk about our homes and our past and tried to tell our friends what our lives had been like. We told what to us were amusing stories of family events, grand occasions and special treats. I am sure we boasted, and must have embroidered and exaggerated. The others enjoyed tales of my siblings. I came from the largest family, and there was plenty I could relate, especially about my older brother Werner, who was rarely out of mischief. The girls heard how Werner had to take his turn in drying the dishes when Mina was washing up. It was a duty he did not relish, and so to irritate and to vent his frustration he said with every object that he dried, 'Where does this go?'

Mina's patience was never elastic. She snapped, 'Hang them in the apple tree!' Werner did not have to be told twice. He rushed into the garden and with simian speed clambered into the tree and disposed of the dishes. Mina was aghast. Werner was told to bring everything down. Smirking, he refused. Mina had to resort to pleading and bribing him with offers of specially cooked treats. Then Werner relented and obliged. In this way the hostel girls managed to find out much about each other and, I think, to care.

Bed-time was hard in the dormitories. We all felt low then, and I know that the heads that slid under the blankets did so to hide the weeping. We did not wish to impose our grief on each other, nor could we expect comfort. We knew that we all shared the same pain, but it was unmentionable. I remember learning to suppress all sound while crying, but I could not control the tears. They just seemed to flow. Night after night I promised myself that I would halt the tears, but the overwhelming feeling of separation repeatedly brought despair. I kept my little photo album, which Mother had so thoughtfully tucked into my belongings, under my pillow. I hoped it would help, that I would feel the family nearer to me, but I was too rooted in reality to delude myself.

I had been taught to say a bed-time prayer as a child, and I prayed fervently, almost wanting to make a pact with God, promising that I would be especially good so that I would deserve a reunion with all the members of my family, a tough assignment for God as we were by then scattered in five different locations over four countries of three separate continents. God's task was to become more difficult still when in 1941 our number on the famous US quota was about to come up for immigration. At that point, my parents and their six children lived in eight different locations: four in France, two in England, one in Argentina and one in the USA.

Personal witness of prayer is difficult to discover. Children do not talk about it, are embarrassed and forget, especially when prayer has not been answered. In the *Mémorial de la Déportation des Juifs de France*,* Serge and Beate Klarsfeld, the editors, copied a child's plea addressed to God. The seven-year-old boy had written it at Drancy, the infamous assembly point near Paris, where French and foreign Jews in France were collected before being deported to Auschwitz and other death camps. Perhaps he lost it before being bundled into a train. There were thousands of children there, many without their parents, who had already joined the transports to the east. This little boy's address to God reads:

> C'est vous qui commandez. C'est vous qui êtes la justice, c'est vous qui récompensez les bons et punissez les méchants. Dieu? Après cela, je pourrai dire que je ne vous oublierai jamais. Je penserai toujours à vous, même aux derniers moments de ma vie. Vous pouvez être sûr et certain... C'est grâce à vous que j'ai eu une belle vie avant, que j'ai été gâté... Dieu? FAITES REVENIR MES PARENTS, MES PAUVRES PARENTS, PROTEGEZ-LES (encore plus que moi-même), QUE JE LES REVOIS LE PLUS TOT POSSIBLE, FAITES-LES REVENIR ENCORE UNE FOIS. Ah! Je pouvais dire que j'avais une si bonne maman et un si bon papa! J'ai tellement confiance en vous que je vous dis un merci en avance.

---

* Maître Serge Klarsfeld, Paris, Beate and Serge Klarsfeld, 1978.

[It is you who command us. It is you who are justice and it is you who reward the good and punish the wicked. Lord? After that I shall be able to say that I shall never forget you. I shall always think of you even in the last moments of my life. You may be sure and certain of it... It is thanks to you that I have had a good life before, that I have been spoilt... Lord? LET MY PARENTS COME BACK, MY POOR PARENTS, PROTECT THEM (even more than you protect me), LET ME SEE THEM AGAIN AS SOON AS POSSIBLE, LET THEM RETURN ONCE MORE. Oh! I could say I had such a good mummy and such a good daddy! I have so much confidence in you that I shall say thank you in advance.]

13 The Priory School, Tynemouth

That first year of the war marked a transition in the lives of all Europeans, and the rest of the world was not unaffected. There was fighting in northern and southern Europe, in the east and in the west. But the German armies found little resistance; they had long prepared for this drive to find more *Lebensraum* ('living space'). Isolated cities, like Rotterdam, had experienced a bout of heavy bombing to make the country submit. The air raids on Britain, particularly on London, had started, and were soon known as the *Blitz*. Language has its own life, and the word changed meaning as the war progressed. The Germans had used the expression with the intention of speed, *Blitz* meaning 'lightning'. It was to be a rapid air attack, a *Blitzkrieg* ('lightning war'), to demoralize the country. Instead, it became the term used in Britain for the ceaseless bombardment of London and other cities.

In Tynemouth too we had an occasional air raid. One had to expect this near the ports. Shipping on the river Tyne and industrial Newcastle nearby were obvious targets. We seemed to be unafraid of bombs. I hated the wailing, grinding sound of the siren more than the explosions or the anti-aircraft gunfire. However, the siren sound of the 'all clear', that we awaited longingly, one long blaring note, was welcome relief.

We attended Priory School. When I visited Tynemouth four decades later, I discovered that the town does indeed boast an ancient ruined

1. Moritz Oppenheimer, my father, was a factory owner and respected employer in the Odenwald.

2. Margarete ('Grete') Oppenheimer, my mother, was a university-educated woman, a mathematician raised in a cultured environment.

3. Mina Dümig, our devout
   Catholic housekeeper, was an
   extraordinarily loyal pillar of
   support. She was like a second
   mother to me.

Darmstädterstraße

Fränkisch-Crumbach i/O.

Schloß

4. The idyllic view of pre-war Fränkisch-Crumbach, as seen on this postcard, masked the social and political turbulence experienced by the village.

5. Our family house, built in 1907 by my father. My father and his first wife Klara are at the window. He was forced to sell it in 1938.

6. Me, aged nine. Last photo in Germany.

7. The Oppenheimer children in 1938 before Werner's departure (clockwise: Werner, Hannah, Ernst, Ruth, Feo and Michael). Our last photo together.

8. With my best friend Elfi (left) in Tynemouth, 1940.

9. My sister Hannah (left) and brother Ernest when we
saw him after years of separation, this time as an
American GI in Europe. (My brother Ernst became
Ernest after he arrived in America.)

10. Hostel Windermere, 1945:
(top row, left to right) Sophie
Goldschmidt, Elfi Reinert, Ruth
Oppenheimer, Lisl Shearer
(Scherzer). Lisl's father had his
name changed from Viennese
Scherzer to English Shearer when
in the Pioneer Corps, hence the
change in Lisl's name also.
(middle row, left to right) Regina
Gutwirth, Ruth Adamecz, Margot
Hirsch, Lore Freitag, Hilde Roth.
(bottom row, left to right) Inge
Adamecz, Ruth Fisch, Lea Roth,
Frieda (Friedchen) Roth.

priory on a headland, bravely facing the onslaught of the North Sea. Ours was a pleasant little elementary school that was somewhat dazed by the invasion of foreign children. We were a puzzle to them, and not only to the pupils. The British of the time were not very well informed about European politics, and it was clear that some teachers had no idea what we 'Germans' were doing there.

Some of the Tyneside children were rougher and tougher than any we had encountered in our previous schools, but they were instinctively kind to us. We were clearly objects of curiosity. Most of them had not met foreigners before and were certainly unused to any tongue but their own. They stood around us and touched us and fired questions. I could never answer any, but my friend Elfi had been there for some months and was spokeswoman. She had been in a class on her own. Not only did she have to learn English, she went at it with a will and was success-ful. I relied on her to do all translations for me, and she obliged. Aged ten, she became the official interpreter that the school used when the rest of us failed, or refused, to understand instructions. Daša would walk out of school when sufficiently bored, quite a brave act at the age of seven.

The local children were even more confused when the war broke out. I do not know what Mr Russell, a kind and good headmaster, told them about us, but possibly enough to make them sorry for children far from home. After 3 September they learnt that all Germans were enemies. Here we were. Germans. Games that had once represented variously named goodies and baddies now inevitably featured these as English and German. What could they make of us? They remained kind, though per-plexed. I distinctly remember one girl who was longing to make friends. She talked and talked at me, and I felt more and more unhappy because I could not respond. Finally, sensing my misery and confusion and as proof of her friendship, she took the sweet that she was sucking out of her mouth and gave it to me. I hope I showed my gratitude by popping it into mine. Joyce Kirkup's gesture is still with me.

In my letters home I wrote that I was beginning to understand what was going on in lessons. Was I lying or was it an attempt to persuade my parents, or perhaps myself, that I was coping? I remember long hours of incomprehension and much tedium.

There were three refugee girls in the top class, the last year of the school, Elfi, Lisl and I. I was allowed to sit next to Elfi, and was quite happy to watch her work. Our teacher, Miss Muir, a Scottish name we found difficult to enunciate, was very strict. She was kind and helpful to us, but we had to obey the rules. We were not allowed to waste time looking at the paintings on the walls during lessons. (The artwork of the children was always posted up, even in the faraway, non-progressive days of my youth.) In my intense boredom I tried to sneak a look at the surrounding walls, but Miss Muir's eyes were all-seeing and I very quickly understood the sense of her commands, if not the words. Pupils were caned on the outstretched hand for minor misdemeanours. This practice was new to me, and I was afraid of having to face the cane. We never did. We tried hard to be good.

I did have one minor success, in art, for which I have little talent. We had been asked to draw and paint a picture about our locality, Tynemouth or Northumberland. The latter, as our county, was far too vast a concept for me, and I had seen nothing of it except Tynemouth, but I did know what Tynemouth meant, on a river and facing the sea. I drew a large fish, filled it with hundreds of scales and tried to apply careful lettering, and without a single mistake wrote, 'THE FISH OF THE TYNE ARE VERY FINE'.

I was proud of my English spelling and of creating a rhyme in this unlearnable language. Miss Muir, with whom I had communicated little, actually smiled at me, a great reward. She did more: with a few flicks of her paintbrush, she applied some rapid curves in real, precious silver paint to the scales of my fish and I experienced a rare moment of bliss.

As a treat for docile class behaviour, Miss Muir would read us *A Tale of Two Cities* by Dickens. I knew the author from reading his work in translation, but had not come across this book. I dreaded it, always, as I understood nothing.

There were some things we could do. Needlework lessons covered a wide range of activities, and we were allowed to knit. All three of us had learnt this at home. Miss Muir saw that Elfi and I were competent knitters, and we were granted permission to knit socks. These marked an advanced and superior target for ten-year-olds, and we derived a sense of unaccustomed pride. Not for long. We knew that Lisl was a mere beginner, and we thought Miss Muir had also noticed this. She must have seen our proud looks vanish as she said Lisl could knit a vest. The similar sounding German word, *Weste*, is 'waistcoat'. That was even more ambitious knitting, we thought. We were asked to bring some suitable wool. Mrs Urbach saw to it that grey was purchased for the socks and dark blue for the 'Weste'. In those days vests, like underwear generally, were a discreet white. Pink might do but was more daring. Miss Muir remonstrated. One did not wear dark blue vests, she told us. Elfi did her best. She had sufficient English to explain that the dark colour selected would not show the dirt as easily as white. Miss Muir gave up. I can see the look today: 'Well, they're foreigners, what can you expect?' it said. Lisl's knitting grew longer and longer and did not seem to be turning into a waistcoat. Eventually we learnt the meaning of 'vest'.

One of the few lessons I actively enjoyed was singing. I did not understand the words of the songs, but they were loud, rousing and patriotic. We launched with gusto into the Welsh 'Men of Harlech', English 'Hearts of Oak' and Scottish 'Bonnie Dundee'. The 'Minstrel Boy' was included to bring home to us that Irish tradition was also part of the British fabric. At a time when 'liberty' was a concept that we understood and recognized, an ideal that few Europeans at the time were able to savour, we sang:

Proudly proclaim, o'er land and sea
This is the home of liberty.
Tyrants beware, ye would but try in vain...

I found it difficult to hide my tears. Our English contemporaries seemed unmoved. It was just one of those songs one had to learn and sing in school. One did not trouble to think about the words. We practised hymns, of which the most moving was William Whiting's:

Eternal Father strong to save
Whose arm doth bind the restless wave.

It had a mighty crescendo of a chorus:

Oh hear us when we cry to thee
For those in peril on the sea.

We understood enough to know that this hymn was profoundly meaningful to the children around us, many of whose fathers were risking their lives at sea, likely to be attacked from above or below. Most of the hymns were not as exuberant as the patriotic songs we were taught at a time of near defeat, but we enjoyed taking part, able at last to share something communal, even if the words we intoned were largely rhubarb. During the daily obligatory religious assembly, for which we practised the hymns, we also learnt to say the Lord's Prayer. While we were actively praying, Mr Cooper, a teacher of lugubrious appearance, walked up and down the rows of children to make sure that our eyes were closed, hands folded and words uttered. Of course, we spoke gobbledygook, though I was sure I had the beginning right, at least. It went, 'Our Father which shout in heaven...' It seemed to make sense. Once I opened my eyes inadvertently to see Mr Cooper looking at me sadly. Was he sorry for me or for the mangled prayer?

In the early spring, English junior schools always prepared their 11-year-olds for an examination called the 'scholarship', later known as the '11-plus'. In the old days of the academic, highly selective grammar schools, children had to pass this test before they could follow courses for the matriculation examination, which led to universities and other academic studies. Much was made of this event, and our teachers prepared us for the three subjects involved: arithmetic, English and intelligence. Any teaching I received in the latter two subjects fell on stony ground. My arithmetic, however, compared favourably with the others. I may have had little schooling, but I had a mathematician as mother and teacher, and I was well taught in this area. When the important day arrived, I was sufficiently intelligent to realize that both intelligence and English were beyond my competence.

But I approached the arithmetic in a positive spirit. I had to do elaborate additions, subtractions, multiplications and divisions, not only with pounds, shillings and pence, but with miles, chains and furlongs, gallons, pecks and bushels. I did not find that difficult. In a forward-looking European way, I decimalized the existing, ancient British system, long before the United Kingdom decided to adopt this rational metric discipline. My instinct told me I had done quite well. I am sure I was accurate. My mother had omitted to teach me that there were 12 pence in a shilling and 240 of them to the pound, not to mention the 22 yards that made up one chain, ten of which were required for a furlong, which with another seven made a mile. It is surprising that English schoolchildren ever found time to learn anything else. Only a few of the English pupils managed to pass the 'scholarship'. I failed with panache.

Priory School was good to us, and provided us with an existence more normal than the daily hostel life. I spent less than a year in that gentle school. Perhaps it closed or someone decided to transfer pupils in the unusual wartime climate. It is possible that numbers had been reduced through evacuation, which had started to take the children away from the east-coast air raids. We were sent to another school, a bleaker place in North Shields grandly called King Edward's. Fortunately for me, I was once again with Elfi, in a large class.

I have happily forgotten the name of our new teacher. She was ill-tempered, we thought. In all the weeks we were with her, she never spoke to us. Did she resent us there as the enemy? Were her loved ones fighting? Had any of them been killed? Was she overwhelmed by the system which expected too much of teachers, as indeed of everyone? I have to admit that she did not look well. Her skin seemed tight across her face, her eyes were sunken, and Elfi and I callously took our revenge by referring to her as the *Totenkopf* ('death head').

Meanwhile in the hostel, tensions and anxieties increased as the war went on. Both matrons and children were worried about relatives left behind. As the Germans invaded the hitherto neutral countries of Europe, we could see our future threatened. What would happen to us if, more likely when, the German armies overpowered England? We were all conscious of the hysterical fear of spies and mistrust of foreigners in Britain. Every non-British citizen was officially declared an alien. For those of us born in Germany or Austria there was the special designation of 'enemy' alien. There were no exceptions. Included were all who had fled the Nazis, even those who had managed to survive the brutality of the concentration camps. We children were not yet affected by the regulations to which adult enemy aliens had to conform; that was not to happen to us until our sixteenth birthday.

But the hysteria did also affect us. Enemy aliens were not permitted to reside near the sea, where they might see war manoeuvres and practices and pass on this information to the Germans. The whole hostel had therefore to be moved away from the area, making control and supervision from the Newcastle committee almost impossible. But before this could happen, many of us were overwhelmed by another scourge, and had to spend much of the summer of 1940 in hospital.

14　Isolation hospital

I n June 1940, a year after my arrival in the hostel, diphtheria, an
epidemic rampant at the time in northeast England, struck the girls,
who were normally in remarkably good health. One after another
we succumbed to the disease, and daily the ambulance took a victim
away. This created a gloomy atmosphere; we always wondered who would
be the next to be carried off by stretcher. We knew that diphtheria was
a serious illness, which could still occasionally be fatal.

Ten girls were sent to hospital. Each one had started by complaining
of a sore throat. A doctor came to take a swab and then we waited for the
results. My English vocabulary increased. I remember learning that swabs
could be 'positive' or 'negative'; also the word 'fumigate'. This was an
official disinfecting procedure, carried out by the local health authority
in the room the last patient had used. We were not allowed to enter
that room, but the smell from outside alone was potent and made the
eyes sting.

Then suddenly no one else was hospitalized. Nine of our companions
had gone. A whole week later, my friend Elfi and I suffered sore throats.
We enjoyed the privacy of our sickness – two in a room was preferable
to a dormitory of ten. It felt good to be apart from the perpetual multitude. We were so rarely alone. The inevitable swabs were taken: hers was
negative, mine was not. Again I had the impression that life was not

always just. The ambulance came and whisked me off to the isolation hospital in North Shields. This time I was not frightened of the unknown. After all, I was the tenth diphtheria victim, and I knew I would be with my friends.

The hospital was bleak and barrack-like, a timber construction. It had been hastily built in the First World War to accommodate some of the many soldiers wounded in trench warfare. Like other temporary public buildings, it had continued to serve. I was carried to a trolley and moved into a large ward with wooden walls and beds in two long rows along each wall. The girls greeted me happily. They were all together there with other young diphtheria patients. Not long after my arrival a nurse came to see to me. She fetched another nurse, who called a doctor. They looked at me, examined my back and chest and the only word I could distinguish from their discussion was the frequently repeated 'doubtful'. I was left alone and asked the others what 'doubtful' might mean. No one really knew, but all were willing to hazard a gruesome guess. We concluded that 'doubtful' was another dire disease.

This guess was not too wide of the mark. 'Doubtful' turned out to be scarlet fever. I had to be isolated. I could not go into a ward with the diphtheria children, nor could I be part of the scarlet fever section. I was an outcast. My conclusion that unfairness ruled was again well on target. As it happened, I did have company for a week in my little side room. Eight-year-old Ivy joined me. She was much loved by the nurses because she sang. Her voice was clear and pure in spite of her sickness, and she sang favourite hits of the day and songs that made fun of Hitler and the Germans, among them,

> We are going to hang out the washing on the Siegfried Line.
> Have you any dirty washing Mother dear?

and

> Underneath the spreading chestnut tree,
> Adolf Hitler said to me,
> If you want a gas mask, don't ask me,
> Ask the blinking ARP.*

---

* Air Raid Precautions, much in evidence at the time.

Both the humour and the English vocabulary were at about my 11-year-old level. Ivy found me very dull. I could not answer her questions even when I vaguely understood them. I assumed she had the same illnesses as I, but she was clearly in the final stages and cheerful because she had been told she was going home soon. If she had been really unwell, her singing would not have been as clear and as forthcoming.

Not that I was very ill. At least I do not remember feeling sick. Before antibiotics, diphtheria was taken seriously, and for the first week we had to lie flat on our backs, without a pillow. Trying to sit up was forbidden. The nurses had to feed and wash us and see to all our needs. After one week, we were given the comfort of a single pillow. By the end of the second week we were allowed two pillows but still no sitting. Three weeks meant a third pillow and permission to sit. After the first week of my eight-week stay, Ivy left and I was alone for the rest of the time. I know that I have never spent any time since or before in which I endured such agonizing boredom. Because I had two diseases I was not allowed the books, toys or puzzles enjoyed by the others. I longed to read, telling myself that if only I had a book, I would suddenly acquire English. It would have been a key to the mystery, I imagined, a Rosetta stone.

The nurses were very busy. They had no time to look in on me, coming only for strictly essential procedures. I knew I could call a nurse for a bedpan, and although this was a temptation I did not have the courage to abuse the privilege. I talked to myself, I cried. When I could bear the situation no longer, I left my bed. I had understood enough English to know that this was a crime, but I was prepared to run the risk for the green view I had from the window. From my bed I could see only clouds, even when I sat up. I was careful, I did not invite discovery. To pass some of the never-ending hours, I managed to make a toy out of a little silver chain I wore. I let it trickle through my fingers and make patterns with it on the sheet. My time in hospital was the nearest experience I could have had to solitary confinement.

June 1940 in Britain was not a good time to be German. There was the calamitous defeat of Dunkirk. The country was on the brink of invasion. Serious air raids had now started over Tyneside. I had the impression that some of the nurses resented us. Like our school companions, they did not understand who we were. As Germans, we were an anomaly. I looked forward to the doctor's visits. He appeared only briefly, as he was indeed busy, but he had some German and sometimes spoke two sentences with me. It meant momentary happiness. The hospital matron, on the other hand, aroused daily dread. In dark green with a frilly white cap, she sailed into and through the wards, a nervous nurse in tow. I soon learned the drill, though not quite as thoroughly as expected. She would ask very formally how I was and I had to answer equally formally that I was very well. I am sure it was the same polite exchange with every patient, well, ill or dying. Unfortunately she succeeded in making me so nervous that I never achieved the correct answer. She tried to teach me daily, and daily I muffed it. In German, in answer to the question, one would say, 'Thank you, very well'. In English, apparently, I had to say it in reverse order, 'Very well, thank you'. Simple enough even for those of limited ability, but I stuttered and invariably produced the wrong version. I knew she would be displeased. But she persevered.

Meal-times should have been diverting. Alas, they were not. In the hostel we were spoiled with food that was well and attractively prepared. Mrs Urbach's culinary skills saw to that. English institutional cooking of those times was at a very low level. For breakfast we had porridge, bread and butter and tea. So far so good. For lunch we ate very liquid minced meat with mashed potatoes, followed by rice pudding. That diet may have been thought out for children with sore throats, so that they would not struggle to swallow. For supper we had rice pudding again. Only. This was the same daily menu for my eight weeks. For children obliged to stay longer, the mince, mash and rice presumably continued. I find it difficult now to believe that anyone could have been so unimaginative. Food rationing had not yet started to grip the country. In fact, rice had to be imported, with merchant-navy seamen risking their lives in convoy ships to bring it from the far-flung empire. They should have been less generous with it.

During my short time with Ivy, I watched with staring envious eyes as she occasionally consumed an egg and cake or biscuits at tea-time. She could feast because her mother brought extras to the hospital, so perhaps the authorities expected our diet to be augmented from home.

At night we could hear the wailing of the air-raid siren which I so disliked. Gunfire and bombs sometimes followed this. We knew that if the attack was close we had to be evacuated to the security of the specially constructed bomb shelter in the grounds. Our wooden building was not safe. If we had to leave, a bell rang shrilly and the nurses came quickly, laid us on the trolleys and wheeled us out. After weeks in bed, we were unable to walk the first time out – except those of us who had already cheated on the regulations.

I looked forward to the shelter outings. Scarlet fever or no, I was able to see my friends and be close enough to them to talk. Once or twice there were loud explosions that silenced us or made us thoughtful, but on the whole we relished the togetherness.

One night there was the usual siren, followed by the bell that signalled evacuation. I heard the nurses scurrying, trolleys with their load of children squeaking along the polished floors, and I was completely confident. I knew I would be one of the last to be fetched, as they emptied the large wards first. To my amazement and disbelief, there was sudden silence. Neither step nor sound in the corridor. Outside, on the contrary, the noise of war was becoming lively. Shocked, I realized they had forgotten me; I was the only one left in the hospital. The idea of solitude worried me more than potential bombs, and I got up. Had I not broken the rules earlier, I would have been quite unable to walk after weeks of being horizontal. As it was, I tottered along the passage and found the main door to the hospital, which I opened. I stood spellbound. The sky was a criss-cross pattern of searchlights, which held me in awe. I could see a plane caught at an intersection of the light beams and I watched in horror and fascination. I knew what this meant. It was not a game. There was much cracking of gunfire, and I remained rigid. Suddenly I heard a voice calling. A nurse had seen me. She came running towards me and dragged me with her to the shelter. The first thing that happened there was a public scolding because I had got up! No one mentioned that *they* had forgotten me. Life again looked unfair.

Eight hospital weeks seemed like a lifetime, but they were over at the very end of July. Surprisingly, we all appeared to be ready to depart on the same day. The reason why we had not left singly as we recovered became clear: the Tynemouth hostel had disappeared. We were not to go back there, but as juvenile enemy had to be taken across the north of England to Windermere in the Lake District, well away from the sea, where we were to live for the next six years. So with this band of young girls gone, Tynemouth and its 'protected' areas, as seaports, military regions and airfields were called, were once again safe.

Once more we faced a journey into the unknown, but we were less apprehensive this time. Pale and thin after our long illness, we at least had the comfort of knowing each other.

15 Windermere

Windermere was to be a surprise. I had not expected to come to a beautiful place. The name was pleasing to start with, and the lake after which the little town is called was gentle-looking and contained, quite unlike the fierce North Sea that I had not learnt to love. And it was quiet. The sea had made a constant noise, especially insistent, sometimes even threatening, at night. The lake was visible from many parts of the village and from near the house that we were to inhabit. Behind the lake the Cumbrian mountains rose, and I soon recognized their special silhouettes, with the twin summits of the Langdale Pikes, the flat curving back of Bowfell and the jagged little peaks of the Crinkle Crags. For the first time in my life I consciously appreciated my surroundings. Was it because the country we now came to know had similarities to the Odenwald? I would not have admitted that at the time, but must confess now that my heart rejoices when I see forests and hills. Are my genes German after all?

The house that was to be our 'home' in both senses was large, part of an estate that had once been called 'The Wood'. It was indeed still near woods and surrounded by trees. A stream flowed through the gardens, which delighted the younger children. In the North Country, streams are known as 'becks', nicely reminiscent of the German 'Bach'. It was a gentler, more country-style house than the tall, somewhat gaunt city building at number 55 Percy Park (which was not a park) in Tynemouth. It was very neglected inside, but had large rooms with one upper floor only and a splendid double staircase. From every window we had a view of trees and shrubs, and a wild meadow that had once been a graceful lawn. It opened up play and withdrawal possibilities and, although we could not have put it into words, a healing closeness to nature. Best of all was a massive tall cedar immediately in front of the house with branches that extended far across the lawn. Ignorant children that we were, we did not know that the cedar was a landmark on local maps, that it had a preservation order on it and was not allowed to be felled. We found this tree a reassuring shelter; at times even protective and comforting. Around the edge of the large garden were thick shrubberies of rhododendrons, azaleas and lilac. Their hidden interior provided custom-built play houses for the younger children, away from adult eyes. There the little ones would play happily at families, invite each other to tea, offering leaves as plates, with wild berries. Shiny beech nuts in abundance provided more make-believe food. In spring our garden wilderness had an abundance of snowdrops to delight us, and later daffodils, bluebells and other wild flowers and a huge, generous magnolia tree.

In spite of the gloomy news on the war front, we all felt some relief at being in Windermere, especially after the cheerless weeks in hospital. There were beautiful mountain and lake views, green everywhere. Air raids were virtually unknown and the occasional wail of the siren was mainly for a harmless practice. The summer holidays were not over, and we did not yet have to face the new school year in an unknown school. There was leisure to explore our unfamiliar surroundings.

One hot August afternoon, the matrons wanted some respite from us and told us to go for a walk, to go to the lake. We dutifully trooped out with towels and bathing suits and found a small road that led to the lake. Some of the older girls could swim, having managed to learn in Germany before the notices went up forbidding Jews entry to swimming pools. They were to look after the younger non-swimmers. We arrived near a group of boathouses. We did not then know that much lake access was private, so no doubt we were trespassing. The older girls happily struck out into the lake, leaving the rest of us playing at the shallow water's edge, in the care of Margot Hirsch, a responsible senior girl, also a non-swimmer. We were playing with a ball, having fun, forgetting our normal anxieties in sunshine and water. Inevitably the ball once went out rather further than intended. Margot, in her dependable way, told us she would retrieve it, we were to stay at the edge. We watched. Suddenly she vanished. What we did not know, when we so lightheartedly approached this lake to play, was that it was in fact a dangerous place, with sudden deep drops and strange underwater rock formations. Margot did reappear briefly, gasping and struggling, clearly out of her depth. How could we rescue her? We were aghast and very frightened.

From my earlier extensive reading I remembered the story of a child who was unable to swim but jumped into the water when needed and suddenly acquired the skill. In theory I also knew the swimming action of arms and legs. So I plunged in after Margot. Like her, I immediately found myself in very deep water and quite unable to swim. I thrashed about, and somehow we came together.

We clung to each other, as if welded jointly, out of sheer instinct and terror. This was the worst thing we could have done, as we were forcing each other downwards. Friend Elfi, alone among the younger children, could swim (her Austrian homeland afterwards learnt to deprive Jewish children of that skill). She swam resolutely towards us, trying to prise us apart and seize hold of us one at a time. Unfortunately in our desperation we attached ourselves limpet-like to her and she could barely free herself, let alone rescue us. Meanwhile the other youngsters were urgently flailing their arms, screaming, trying to attract the swimmers far out in the lake. The older girls thought at first that this was innocent *joie de vivre* and did not immediately return. In later years, Stevie Smith's poem 'Not waving, but drowning' was to have a special meaning for me.

I remember little after that. Margot and I must have drifted apart and were probably losing consciousness, the prelude to loss of life. Today, a lifetime later, I still know very clearly what drowning feels like. There was an intense sensation of being stretched apart. Gravity was pulling my feet with the rest of me downwards and my neck and head were straining upwards, avid for a gulp of air.

I was not aware of my rescue or rescuer. Later I heard that Marion Mendelssohn, still tall, thin and unhappy, had understood that something was amiss and raced across the water towards us. We were told later that she managed to pull us both out. The others were apparently very frightened, wondering whether we had died. I eventually came to, as I felt heavy pressure on my back and water spurting from my mouth, quite beyond my control. A man living nearby, Mr Rothera, had heard the screaming and had appeared. It was he who was pumping water out of me. Margot too recovered, though more slowly. Mr Rothera took us to his house a little way back from the lake. There we had a hot bath and something to drink. Embarrassed as I spluttered, I discovered that my throat muscles did not function. I wanted to thank him but I had no voice, not even a croak. It had totally disappeared.

We were subdued on our way back to the hostel. Margot and I found walking difficult and were inclined to stagger. The older girls had discussed the event and decided that nothing was to be said to the matrons. No one was to know. We were asked how the afternoon had gone and non-committal answers came from those that could speak. At supper I did not feel like eating. One of the girls hissed at me that I had to eat, that if I did not, suspicions would be raised. Obedient, I was promptly sick. In reply to the questions that followed, I was unable to bring forth a single sound, the others explained for me, and the story emerged. The lake is known to be dangerous and seems to take an annual toll. It was clear the matrons felt relieved that we had not died; there might have been unpleasant consequences. But I yearned for the arms that would hug me and reassure me that my survival mattered. Comforting arms were a remembered luxury, not part of hostel life.

We had not thought of ourselves as difficult children. However, I have lived in 'good' neighbourhoods, where local residents are invariably frightened of the influx of a 'different' group. They will object to the setting up of a home for delinquents or for psychiatric patients or ex-prisoners or aliens. If they cannot prevent such a 'downward' social trend, they will at least watch newcomers warily. When we first arrived in our select corner of Windermere, we were not particularly welcome. Had it been otherwise, we would have been astonished. We had two elderly ladies as neighbours, and they were decidedly suspicious of us, and watched our coming and going to see whether we would pick their flowers, which grew in great profusion along the drive that led to

'Southwood', the name of the hostel. Other neighbours were never directly unfriendly, but preferred to ignore us. They must have feared that we would let down the tone of a genteel area.

Gradually Miss Stella and Miss Elsie Hamilton at 'Brackenfold', next door, smiled at us, and we returned their smiles. Then they spoke to us, and eventually a real friendship was established. Two years later they even gave a Christmas party for us in their lovely home. They taught us English children's games. They spoiled us with a splendid festive spread, in spite of stringent food rationing by then. They had a little gift wrapped for each of us. We thought they were wonderful, and so they were.

Not all neighbours were like that. Take Mrs Hargreaves: our friend Edith Rossmann, whom we envied because she had an accessible mother in England, eventually left the hostel because her mother, with the financial help of English friends, had been able to send Edith to Kendal High School (also in the Lake District). It was an academic school and Edith's mother, anxious, poor and helpless, still managed to remove Edith from the hostel because she wanted Edith to be able to take advantage of the new school and to study, which she could not do in the hostel. Mrs Rossmann was employed in a domestic job not far from the hostel. Mrs Urbach and Mrs Sieber did not approve of a mother living so near, and did not seem to care that Edith left. As a domestic worker, Mrs Rossmann only had a tiny room with a single bed. This now had to do for mother and daughter. But Elfi and I missed Edith. We had been fond of her. We were resourceful girls. After all, our friend lived only a short distance away. She would often pass along the road from which a drive led to the hostel. We wanted to stay in touch, although this was not allowed. Edith was meant to be in a state of disgrace.

Like much of northern England, Windermere is well supplied with ancient dry-stone walls, as was our Patterdale Road. What could be easier than to write messages to Edith, take out a small stone from the wall, hide our scrap of paper in the crevice and replace the stone? We even marked it with chalk so that Edith would find it easily. This worked for a few days. We had noticed Mrs Hargreaves standing at her window at 'Northwood', part of the Wood estate on which we also lived. Mrs Hargreaves did not approve of us, and never smiled when we met her. Even seeing her at her observation post, we remained unworried.

Not long after, the police arrived at the hostel. It had been reported that two girls (we were 11 and 12 respectively) were putting secret messages into a wall. This was wartime, and they wanted to interview us. The assumption clearly was that they had to investigate the possibility of German espionage. Our note had said: 'How are you? We are fine. Mrs Urbach is horrible. We miss you.' Secret code, no doubt. We owned up immediately when asked to come forward. Not much point in denying anything. Mrs Hargreaves would happily have picked us out of a group in an identity parade.

What did anyone imagine we could have been up to? What was there to report in Windermere? What secret agents would have been sauntering along the Patterdale Road to pick up our secrets? Of course Edith, aged 14, could have been a spy too. But it was not the forbidding policeman interviewing us who struck terror in our hearts. It was the prospect of Mrs Urbach's reaction to our note.

There was, however, one ill-kept war secret in Windermere, which everyone seemed to know, even the enemy aliens. Down on the lake shore, near Troutbeck Bridge between Windermere and Ambleside, was a factory that made Sunderland Flying Boats. We would occasionally see a plane take off from the lake to fly for a while over the hills, and then land gracefully back on the water. These planes were a dazzling white and on a blue day looked beautiful on the lake. Did anyone think that we of all people would, or knew how to, let the Germans have this secret?

That first year in Windermere provided me with an unexpectedly happy event. My good Aunt Liese, working with her domestic permit in York, managed to save enough money from her very modest wages as a cleaner to buy rail tickets for Hannah in the South of England and me in the North to be reunited with her, half-way, or almost. The railway journey was an ordeal. Travelling alone at 11, I feared I would be recognized as German. When anyone looked at me, wondering perhaps why a young girl was travelling on her own, I avoided their attention by carefully looking out of the window, anxious not to be addressed. My English was certainly not up to explanation or disguise. I even had to change trains twice at busy junctions, Carnforth in Lancashire and Leeds in Yorkshire. I seemed to manage, though I was neither brave nor hopeful.

This was the first time I was to meet close relatives after having been forced to leave the secure family net, and I was afraid. No doubt Hannah was feeling the same as my train approached. My aunt and Hannah were both there to meet me at York station, a vast Victorian edifice not unlike the last station I had seen in Frankfurt, a place that would forever haunt me. For years to come, stations were to be places of tension and anxiety for me. My aunt looked much as she had always looked, so continental-European, so non-English. Her sensible raincoat, in which I remembered her so well, was grey and very much longer than the fashion in England at the time. Her unstylish, German, round felt hat was pulled straight down her head, leaving only her plaited bun exposed. Hannah was beside her, coatless and hatless, hair flying, with a happy grin on her face. As we hugged, we were tearfully happy but initially awkward with each other. My aunt's usual transport was the bicycle, but at York station we waited for a bus. I was longing to see her home on the outskirts of the city, which she shared with Mrs Schwarzwald, a refugee friend from Frankfurt. The very idea of being in a private house, actually living there for a while, away from the crowd we always associated with, was happiness. We were not disappointed. The house was a tiny bungalow, with front and back garden. It was furnished simply with the few good pieces that the friend had managed to ship across. There were some pictures of German mountain and forest landscapes as well as an old print of the 'Römer', the oldest part of the city of Frankfurt. Such a warm reminder of home. My aunt, neither a country woman nor a gardener, had taken happily to the soil. The front of the house displayed a multitude of flowers and the back proved that she had taken the national slogan 'Dig for Victory!' to heart. Vegetables stood in Prussian rank and order. Not only were the two ladies able to feed themselves, they also provided for the neighbours.

Hannah and I had changed, perhaps I more than Hannah. She had always been taller than her age group, and did not seem to have grown much more. I, as the younger child, had developed physically in the intervening time. It seemed a new relationship. This was partly because our 14 months separation meant we discovered a new sibling link, forged through our loss and longing, far removed from the wary state of un-declared war we had sometimes felt in the past. We had both faced a new life that we had not chosen, new experiences we had neither looked for nor expected. She now treated me less as the irritating little sister who had annoyed her so much. I was more of a real person. We each represented the family for the other, a bond with better times, even if we had spent much of our young lives quarrelling. We both glowed when we saw signs of the old humour and the fun that sometimes surfaced again. But our past and our family were not a topic for conversation. We stuck to the present. Even the future was too hazardous to think about. Our aunt did her utmost to make us happily at ease. We relished hearing her Frankfurt German (Germans are much prouder of local accents than are Britons or Americans), which reminded us of Mother's, and we cheerfully lapsed into our own, slightly different Odenwald dialect. We relaxed and felt accepted, at home. I did have fantasies about living with my aunt, and I am sure she would have been glad to take us for her sister's sake, but for a single working woman with a pittance as wages it would have been impossible. She never lost her love of German literature, and read us poems by Friedrich Stolze written in the Frankfurt dialect, just as Mother used to do. These were mainly satirical but also contained broad, even coarse humour of the type children can understand and relish. Because we could remember many of the poems and stories, we wallowed in the familiar and the revisiting of past pleasures. To our delight, Aunt Liese had brought books from Germany when she emigrated, and we threw ourselves at them and immersed ourselves in the gothic script and nineteenth-century comic, sometimes even scurrilous, illustrated verse tales of Wilhelm Busch. I certainly did not understand the satirical innuendoes of 'Die Fromme Helene' ('Pious Helen'), but the fact that our mother had read them with happy laughter was incentive enough for me to enjoy them also. Our aunt did her best to encourage us. We laughed till we cried, grateful for the luxury of tears of joy.

After that long summer of 1940, we started at a new school. This was St Mary's Girls, Windermere, an old-fashioned, somewhat underprivileged little church elementary school, separated from St Mary's Church only by the cemetery. This school too had kind teachers, overwhelmed by the number of pupils, far too many for the size of the place. But it was wartime, as we were constantly reminded, and one had to 'take the rough with the smooth', an English phrase I learnt early, though there was little evidence of the smooth. That summer, as a result of the air raids on Tyneside, whole schools were evacuated from Newcastle and other places on the northeast coast, westwards to the Lake District. This was not only further from the bombs but also from an all-too-likely invasion, an ever-present fear. St Mary's doubled in size with the influx of a South Shields school and some of its teachers.

There must have been chaos, but on the whole we were not aware of it. The teachers tried very hard to fit us all into the already overfilled classes. Miss Margaret Webster was the headmistress of the Windermere school. She was a small, slender, almost wispy little lady who never raised her voice, but organized efficiently, taught full-time, and cared. We came to love and appreciate her. She seemed especially good to us, the refugees. She coped with the swollen numbers, the presence of the rival head-mistress from South Shields, the vicar of St Mary's Church to which the school was attached, the boiler that tried and failed to heat the school, and the numerous new wartime regulations.

It cannot have been an easy school, with so many evacuees out-numbering the local children. Some of them were not happy in families that had been forced to take them in. Most Windermere households had extra people billeted. Local gossip had it that they preferred children from Tyneside to the cockneys from London. At least the Tynesiders had the merit of being northerners.

Like much of Windermere, St Mary's Church and the school were built in Victorian neo-Gothic. Inside it was decidedly primitive by twentieth-century standards. There was one large hall, divided into three classrooms by screens. These were too tall for children to peep over, but teachers' heads could suddenly appear. Miss Webster had her head-mistress desk at one end of the room and taught her 'top' class, the seniors, there. As I stayed at that end of the room between the ages of 11 and 14, I assume she had three classes together in her third of the room. It must have been nerve-wracking for the other two teachers behind the further screens that their headmistress could hear every word of what was going on. So could we. There was a boiler/stove against the wall mid-room, but the heating was not effective. The pointed, arched windows were all well above our heads, so that there should be no temptation to look out into the open. The lavatories were in the yard, not water but earth closets, and I trained myself never to use them for the next three years. I considered that an achievement. There were three small hand basins for the whole school, cold water only, just inside the main entrance.

In the melee of the beginning of term, with numbers doubled, the school still managed to take care of the foreigners, who had mostly failed to understand the stream of instructions. Our names and ages were noted and we were dispatched to classes. Elfi and Sophie were to go to the top class. I, six months younger than Elfi, was to be behind a screen in the middle of the room. Panic. I did not want to face separation from Elfi. I knew exactly what was required of me, but I pretended that I could not understand English sufficiently well and stood my ground, that is close to my friend. No persuasion would make me budge. Finally they gave up and I had my way.

Even before the overcrowding, the curriculum of the school had been excessively simple. Educational facilities were few. We had no gymnasium, so we did jerky, physical exercises in the paved yard. We learnt simple history and geography; English, which Miss Webster loved and taught well; arithmetic, starting daily with a 'mental' dose; occasional painting, and needlework every afternoon. On dark days this was a chore, as we had no electricity in the building. Our gentle light was gas, with lamps fixed to the walls. Those of us in the middle of the room could see only little. As it was a church school, scripture was taught every morning, usually by the vicar from next door. By then someone had suggested that we, as Jewish children, should not attend prayers and scripture. I was sorry about that, as I wanted to conform to the norm. I cannot imagine that we might have been persuaded to convert our sketchy religious beliefs into another sketchy credence as a result of such attendance. During the scripture hour, the refugees had to be occupied.

Wartime regulations had instituted free milk for all children. In sophisticated urban schools this milk arrived in small bottles with straws. No such luxury in Windermere. The local farmer brought the milk in churns, more or less straight from the cow, fresh and delicious. Our job was to measure out this milk, to pour it into individual cups the children had brought from home, to carry trays of filled cups carefully to each classroom, and to wash and scald with water specially boiled in large kettles the churns and all the implements we had used. We enjoyed our new self-importance. It was not always possible to do this job totally silently, and occasionally we clattered or chattered too loud. The vicar, Mr Harland, was easily irritated and displeased with us. Was it just our inability to complete our task in silence, or was it that we were exceptions and not in his class? I was glad when I heard later that he had been elevated to become Bishop of Durham.

16 Adolescence in Windermere

Memories of the next few years merge. The longer the war lasted, the more anxious we became about those we had left behind. The matrons found life with us increasingly frustrating. They had expected to do this job for six months to a year. Our parents were supposed to come and fetch us, take us elsewhere and relieve the committee of a great financial headache and the matrons of an onerous task, for which they were scarcely suited. Since the move from the northeast coast to the other side of the country, the members of the Newcastle committee were not as readily available with their moral support, advice and encouragement. Mrs Urbach and Mrs Sieber became less tolerant of us, but the adolescent rebellion that surged in our being had to be contained. We endeavoured to hide such signs of mutiny. The passing years no doubt spelled uncertainty and loss for the matrons also. We were all in limbo, knowing that the hostel must come to an end some day. But when? And what then? Gradually the older girls left. There was plenty of work available. By the time we had reached Windermere, only the middle ones and younger children attended school.

The big ones, as we continued to call the eldest group of girls, found outside employment. They had realized that with their education in Germany truncated for most of them, and the British school-leaving age at 14, they had missed out on the kind of schooling that most of us, from our relatively educated backgrounds, would have acquired, had Hitler never appeared on the scene. Some girls were quite enterprising. Eva Less had the good sense to leave for work in Lewisham Hospital (London), a well-known provider of a good nursing training. She did not seem sad to leave the hostel or Windermere, she showed relief.

Paula Katz, like Eva originally from Berlin and very much a sophisticated city girl, left for the 'land army' to do heavy agricultural work. For her this was by no means an ideal solution – none of us had forgotten the scarlet fingernails – but she too yearned for an escape route.

Ilse Gross, so fortunate to have a mother employed in Windermere, moved into sparse attic accommodation to live with her. I know we younger ones who visited the place thought it was heaven to have one's 'own' home, and would have been happy to put up with the meanest living conditions with any member of our family. Ilse showed enterprise from an early age, and speedily found work. She was resourceful. Like the rest of us, she had imperfect English, but charm, self-confidence and powers of persuasion ensured her employment in Windermere at Boots the Chemist. If her English was inadequate for the recommendations and knowledge required of a librarian, she was not going to let that block her entry to the Boots lending library. Discriminating ladies liked to select their reading there in those days. It seems an unlikely venture for a pharmaceutical firm, but Ilse acquitted herself well there.

Margot Hirsch became an apprentice to a ladies' hairdresser, glad to be learning a trade and to have the opportunity to be out of the house and the constant watchful gaze of the matrons. Annie found work in a Windermere dress shop. She was happy and accepted there, was thanked for her services and treated as a younger sister by the ladies in charge, quite different from the hostel, where her sewing and the drudgery of remaking old clothes for the rest of us was taken for granted.

By then the country seemed to have waived the prohibition on work for refugee children. With so many men and women in the armed services, a workforce was needed for ordinary jobs. If they were not working outside the hostel, the girls had to do the cooking, cleaning and sewing inside. As the rest of us grew up, we all had jobs to do in the house. Some girls even learnt to cook from Mrs Urbach, and rightly considered themselves fortunate. One had to be a favourite for that privilege. I was not selected, but became an efficient dish-washer and potato peeler.

As a Viennese girl, Elfi was always a favourite of Mrs Urbach. The fact that she was also biddable and accepting did not go amiss either. Elfi had learnt early in life to ignore the injustices that abounded and not to complain. She was of course right. It would not have done her any good. She told me later that Mrs Urbach informed her of the facts of life. I do not know whether any other girls were considered worthy of such esoteric knowledge, but Elfi, ever discreet, did not share her new-found wisdom. Perhaps she had been told it was only for her.

Marion Mendelssohn, who had saved me from drowning, had also gone. In her case not to work but to become a patient in a psychiatric hospital in Preston, in those days still known as an asylum. Since she had come to England at the age of 13, she had certainly suffered from severe depression, though that is not what we called it then. She rarely laughed. Her blue eyes looked dull and unfocussed. We were told that she had been asked to go as she had apparently committed theft. I remember the circumstances only vaguely. A purse was missing. Marion was accused of stealing it. I do not know whether she had found it or whether it was found among her few possessions. I do, however, have a vivid picture in my mind of a dramatic scene, with Marion on her knees in front of Mrs Sieber, sobbing as she begged forgiveness. Such emotional outbursts were not unknown in our hostel life. Mrs Sieber herself was not above a dramatic pose or two. She would clutch her head in disbelief at some girl's behaviour, or throw out her arms in a state of excitement. At the time I knew little about psychological problems or attention-seeking behaviour. To me, as a child, theft was theft and a crime. The matrons unfortunately were as ignorant as I. They did not understand our needs, our behaviour or even our deep unhappiness. The prevalent idea at the time was that 'children forget', should 'get over their misery', that it was 'best not to talk about it'. How convenient that would have been. Marion left, and we were not to hear from or about her again until we found her in Western Australia half a century later. I do not like to imagine what her life must have been like in the asylum, though I hope she found people there who understood and cared.

Another girl, whom we did not know well, as she had not arrived in the hostel before the war when the rest of us came, joined us after we had moved to Windermere. Lia (Cornelia) Stadtler, a 14 or 15-year-old adolescent originally from Prague, had been with an English foster family in Gateshead after leaving her native city. The family apparently did not want her any more, and asked the Newcastle committee to take her on. She was sent to join us, a fresh-faced, jolly girl who liked to do her own thing. She was not to be with us for very long. One day she disappeared. When she returned some hours later, too late in the evening I imagine, it was discovered that she had gone out with a soldier. She was expelled. I do not know where she landed, and I think none of us dared ask.

Of course boys or young men were not part of our lives. We simply never met any. Today I find it curious that we did not spend time talking about boys, even imaginary ones. Perhaps the topic was taboo, like others that we had learnt not to mention. Our Windermere Church of England school was for girls only. We lived away from the village, isolated and surrounded by woods. The boys' school was about a mile away. We did occasionally see Peter, Mrs Sieber's son. He was no longer a boy, but a handsome young man in a naval uniform, doing dangerous work on a minesweeper. He would come to visit occasionally when he was off duty, and there was great rejoicing in the house. Of course Mrs Sieber was relieved and particularly happy and Mrs Urbach was willing to prepare culinary treats for the hero. This meant a good time for us all, as the happy atmosphere lightened our gloom. Most of the girls adored him and the younger ones among us discovered with giggles and glee that all the big ones were in love with him. I found it difficult to understand that. After all I was used to boys, I had three brothers, two of whom were now young men themselves. I could not see what was so special about this young man. It was difficult to believe that some girls might fall in love with my own brothers, unimaginable really for a 12-year-old.

We met two more boys over the years. One of our favourite committee members, Mrs Freedman from Newcastle, had two sons, both about the age of the older girls. They occasionally spent holidays in Windermere to get away from the air raids over Tyneside. Their parents had found a small house, Westwood, at the back of our Southwood. (These, with Eastwood and Northwood, were subdivisions of the original grand house.) The Freedman boys, Huntly and Roland, also caused a considerable flutter among the hostel inmates. I do not think they were interested in us. They surely knew more exciting and sophisticated young ladies through connections in their home town. I considered myself immune, though I remember that I once tried to help catch frogs, creatures that Roland, a medical student, required for his biology classes. I cannot imagine why I would volunteer to do that – I was afraid of touching animals. Perhaps I too was somewhat smitten.

The hostel was supported and totally financed by the Jewish committee of Newcastle, which expected our establishment to be run on orthodox, religious lines. The matrons either did not know how to do this, perhaps being unfamiliar with orthodox practices, or found the process too irksome. Some girls came from orthodox backgrounds, others did not. I noticed that sometimes we had to pretend to cook, clean and behave according to orthodox tradition, and in my early adolescent priggish manner I felt this was dishonest. Unfortunately I said so. Mrs Sieber did not hesitate. She struck me hard across the face. That was the first time I was hit. No doubt I spoke my mind in a surly, graceless way. I had muttered something about hypocrisy. I did not know this English word at the time, but knew the German, which again is much more immediate in its significance and easy even for inexperienced children: 'Scheinheilig' ('seemingly holy'). It fitted well.

Lore was not the only child who was beaten, though in her case it was a regular event, as her intense unhappiness at leaving home at the age of five had provoked her enuresis. This involuntary bedwetting was to dog her for a long time, with the usual consequences. No wonder she was traumatized. In later life, knowing that she was dying of cancer, she wrote her story for the benefit of family and friends in New Zealand. She does not describe her beatings and the reason for them, but does dwell on her trauma: 'Coming from a warm and loving home to a harsh impersonalized institution was indeed a traumatic experience for me as a six-year-old. I felt alone, afraid and always cold. I have clear recollections of having frequent temper tantrums and being sent to bed where I would cry myself to sleep.' She also wrote, 'The girls would be severely punished for the slightest misdemeanour. A crumb left on the table would be enough to trigger off a ROW, one of the first words in my English vocabulary. It was usually Mrs Urbach's booming voice echoing through-out the house, delivering a slap on the face against indignant cries of the poor victim.'

Lea, the youngest of the three little Roth girls, and indeed the very youngest inmate of the hostel, describes beatings on bare buttocks. These three little girls were very different. Hilde was ever serious. She accepted her responsibilities towards the two younger ones, Frieda and Lea. She did not easily relax or smile. She rarely let her attention wander away from her charges. She often looked weary and years older than she was. The middle sister, Frieda, was known only by her diminutive name in German, 'Friedchen', which means something more than just 'little Frieda'; it carries the additional flavour of 'sweet', or 'dear'. And that was how we all viewed her. Friedchen had gorgeous dark brown eyes with the longest black eyelashes, and soon learnt to flutter them to good effect. Everyone was entranced. She did not have to do anything else to earn attention, she did not need to utter any words, though occasionally she would reward us all with a tiny shy smile. She became everyone's pet. The matrons made their choice of favourites very clear too. Friedchen stayed a pet for a long time, until she fell out of favour, as inevitably happened. (That may have been a worse fate than never being in favour.) Even favourite children can have a tiresome side. What was most unfor-tunate was that Lea, our youngest, soon knew that she was not a little pet, that she did not have entrancing looks. She was actually told by Mrs Urbach, 'You are such a sour little girl! Why can't you be like your sister Frieda?', a ploy not designed to turn Lea charming or biddable. The little ones had more physical abuse than the rest of us. It would have been difficult to subject older and bigger girls to beatings, though sudden blows were not unknown. Ruth Adamecz too remembers the unexpected slaps. When once she and her sister Inge were in a bath together, still quite young, as Mrs Urbach was apparently present in the bathroom, the latter asked them with some interest, 'What do you want to do when you are grown up?' Ruth, conscious of her talents and artistic longings, said simply, 'I would like to be an artist,' whereupon Mrs Urbach pulled her out of the bath, slapped her and called her 'bohemian', presumably intending this as an insult. Perhaps artist life in Vienna was 'bohemian' and did not fit with current bourgeois morals.

Aware of the hostility that I now felt directed towards me, I found it easier to speak out and say that things were 'unfair', a word that was to play a major part in my troubled hostel life. As a tall and strong adolescent, I never suffered the beatings that some of the little ones endured, but I often caught a stinging blow. One episode in particular has stayed with me.

Since our Eton crop days, I was sensitive about my hair, and I always put off cutting it. Long hair was not approved in those days; it implied untidiness and loose living, and Mrs Urbach suggested I should have a 'Mozartzopf' ('Mozart-plait'), a ponytail. I was unable to visualize such a hairdo, but could imagine that Mozart had plaited his hair to keep it out of the way and off his sheet music as he composed. Mrs Urbach was prepared to demonstrate in front of a mirror. It was simply a tying back of the hair the way many a young man in total unawareness of Mozart might sport his locks now, but mine was to be tied with a bow. I did not care for that kind of adornment, nor did I want a change in my appearance, but lacked the courage to refuse. However, Mrs Urbach could see by my expression in front of the mirror that I did not appreciate the new coiffure. With sudden anger she struck me hard across the face. This confirmed to me once and for all what I had felt for a long time. She disliked me intensely. In the looking glass, I saw the dark red impression of her hand on my cheek, and felt a burst of fierce hatred for her. Thereafter our dislike for each other became permanent. Her angry eyes bored into me, and my sullen expression was an attempt at defiance. But we had to live together.

Some months later came a difficult decision, and I braced myself to reveal to Mrs Urbach a matter of deep personal significance and an embarrassment for a 13-year-old girl. I had started menstruation. 'So what?' she snapped at me.

We were mostly utterly ignorant of any of the facts of life. I had vague ideas about menstruation, as older girls complained about it. The only word that we used to describe the condition was the one we had been taught: *Unwohl* ('unwell'). We knew we were not unwell, but we also knew that the topic was unmentionable. It was secret, perhaps even dirty. Disposable sanitary towels did not exist, and we had to deal with our soiled ones by wrapping them discreetly in old newspaper – only a little paper, as in wartime that too was a precious commodity. Then they were to be burnt in the boiler that heated our hot water, which was in the kitchen. Because of the shame attached to being *unwohl*, we tried to sneak into the kitchen when it was empty. This was not always easy, and so occasionally we hid the little package in our bedside locker, our only private place. Unfortunately this was not always private. An inspection of our lockers and the single drawer we each had was sprung upon us every now and then, of course always without warning. They wanted to ensure that we were clean and tidy everywhere at all times. Occasionally our dirty secrets were revealed. I too was guilty, and again I was hit.

There was a false modesty in operation. We did not readily undress in front of each other, but dressed and undressed under our nightwear. Most of us had no objections to nudity, but knew that it was undesirable, even vulgar. A bedroom of Southwood, the name of the original house, had been turned into a bathroom, and because there were at least 20 of us when we moved, two baths, three washbasins and two lavatories had been installed there. The baths were separated by a curtain, the lavatories walled in with flimsy plywood open at top and bottom. It was easy for the occupants of the lavatories to converse, a major misdeed that ensured furious scolding. Those caught were reminded that they must have come from an undesirably vulgar background. In our homesick state that was especially hurtful. Rightly or wrongly we idealized our original homes, and criticism of these homes left a wound.

I was not the only girl at odds with our matrons. Perhaps this happens in a closed community, but we soon realized that there was frequently one girl who became a focus of victimization. Everything was wrong with her for a time, and she was constantly in trouble, accused of quite minor misdeeds. Sophie, Lisl, Daša and the Adamecz sisters were all targeted in turn with vindictive criticism. Daša, for example, caught Mrs Urbach's heavy hand for hanging up her coat with a sleeve inside out. All our sins which attracted her blows were of the same order. Like many of us, Daša continued to be afraid of Mrs Urbach. She dreaded the stubby, arthritic finger that would point at her accusingly, always followed by a stormy tirade. Since then, she declares today, when anyone points a finger in her direction she shudders. Children are aware of adult foibles.

Sophie's unhappiness compelled her into the Windermere Post Office to draw her savings, all of £2, hardly a fortune even in those days. From there she went to the railway station to run away to London. Elfi and I chanced upon her and ran back to the hostel. We had no choice, we had to betray her. London in wartime and under bombardment was not a safe option for a 14-year-old lonely girl. Our self-righteousness at the decision was not dimmed by Sophie's resentment.

We each had private anxieties that we could not discuss with others. Margot was deeply unhappy that we did not obey all the orthodox Jewish laws to which she was accustomed from her parental home. She wept often on Friday evenings when she remembered the fervour and joy with which her family had celebrated the eve of Sabbath. To her we desecrated not only the Sabbath but Jewish life itself. It was as if by ignoring her faith we were further endangering her family.

In an effort to raise some extra money for the hostel, the Newcastle committee had the idea of inviting Jewish girls from London to live with us as paying guests during the summer holidays, to give them a respite from the city's heavy bombardment. Three girls came to stay while their parents spent part of the summer holiday in a local hotel. We resented them, partly because we had to treat them as special guests, making obvious the difference between them and us, partly because they had parents close by, and most of all because they could look on their time in the hostel as the briefest interlude in what we knew must be happy family lives.

Another communal activity was to help the 'war effort', for which we were sent out in groups to collect nature's gifts, nettles for example. I cannot imagine what their use might have been, but they were not easy to gather. We picked foxgloves too, a weed in the Lake District, for their medicinal digitalis content, and rosehips, a most useful source of vitamin C, we were told. Apparently babies were grateful for the syrup made from these berries. The wild briar rose flourished, and in spite of the thorns, picking the brilliantly shiny orange and scarlet hips was fun. We enjoyed these outings.

Less thrilling was the picking of blackberries. We were expected to fill buckets, which took many hours. It was the wild variety, therefore smaller than the commercially available fruit, with a strong if some-what sour taste. As a little girl, I had occasionally picked blackberries with Mother or Mina, and was quite proficient. As we were expected to gather so many, we often had to stay out for hours performing this chore, which became very tedious as the level of fruit increased so slowly, the scratches from the thorns more rapidly. Nor were we supposed to eat while picking. Not that we were controlled, but if we ate too many the evidence would show around mouths and on tongues or handkerchiefs.

Fuel for heating the house was in very short supply, so we were sent to gather wood. This was a task that all little ones and middle ones were obliged to do, sometimes twice or thrice a week. As it was a winter duty, there were times when we were very cold. We had to go into the nearby woods and gather sticks for kindling, but also any larger branches that we could break and carry in sacks, or on a wide canvas sheet which four girls, one at each corner, carried along the narrow paths and negotiated over the dry-stone walls while trying not to lose any of the precious load. Sometimes this provoked hilarity, more often frustration. Apart from the damp cold, we enjoyed these outings. There was an unaccustomed feeling of freedom. The woods felt friendly, in spite of our associating them with tales of Hänsel and Gretel, Little Red Riding Hood and the babes that were lost. Many of us suffered chilblains, painful, itchy, red swellings on hands and feet. These were apparently the result of cold and vitamin deficiencies. No one ever said thank you for our effort, however much we tried to find the best fuel or vast quantities of wild berries, nor was praise considered a necessary part of our upbringing. It should have been part of the good manners that we were ourselves taught to acquire. We did not complain much. There was the ever-present unspoken thought that those who were dear to and far from us were probably suffering much more.

At one point in the war, a group of us was asked to help a fund-raising effort for the Red Cross or some other wartime charity. We had to stand at different spots in Windermere village rattling a tin can, smiling sweetly. I did not look forward to this. I knew I was incapable of asking for money, even by shaking a tin. As for smiling, how could I do that to strangers? A hostel child, I had no right to refuse – who was I, after all? Unwillingly I eventually stood at a corner, looking miserable, glaring at people as if to dare them to put pennies into my tin. Certainly no charity could depend on my contribution. In spite of the unattractive sight I presented, some people, perversely, contributed. The moment of reckoning arrived. When all the money was counted, mine was by far the smallest amount.

To the matrons this was further proof: I lacked charm and grace. I would 'never find a husband'. As we moved further into our teens a husband naturally seemed the vital solution to our future, a distant hope. But in my case, no hope at all. Yet I really did not want a husband who was looking for Viennese-style charm. For me any man approved by the matrons was likely to be as much of a nightmare as they.

Nineteenth-century ideas of proper behaviour manifested themselves in more concrete ways. In a letter from her father in Germany, sent via a third country, our friend Sophie had news of her mother's sudden death. This was the first time we heard of one of our own parents dying, and it shocked us deeply. Frau Goldschmidt was probably the only one of our parents, as far as we shall ever know, who was not killed, who mercifully had a natural death. For most Jews there would be a prayer for the dead ('Kaddish') but that was not part of the ritual in the hostel. Sophie at 13 was put into mourning. This was considered correct procedure: an outward show. I do not remember that she ever wore black, but she was dressed in the same grey frock for many weeks, if not months, an ever-present reminder of her loss. I felt at the time that this was cruel. She did not need to be marked out in mourning attire. How could she forget her mother?

We were all subdued by Sophie's misfortune. Our unspoken anxiety was increased. When would we have similar news?

17 French connections

The war continued. It seemed endless. News was still the most important event in our lives. When the matrons listened to the BBC broadcasts, we were also able to listen. We gradually understood more English, though at times our frustration was intense, when through lack of language we missed some vital information. As children we were possibly better informed of the progress of the war than others of our age. European place names meant more to us, as did the maps printed in the newspapers. We also understood that German military success spelled disaster for us, a disaster we would rather have faced with our families than separated from them.

Sometimes, if no one was watching, we twiddled knobs on the radio till we heard German spoken. It was still our most familiar language. It could be from the BBC's World Service programmes, which broadcast to Germany. At other times we knew we were hearing a Nazi broadcast by the clipped tones barking invective against the Allies, with constant interruptions of insistently martial music. The music was familiar; we had heard it often in Germany. The staccato notes of the Horst Wessel song, signature tune of the Nazi party, still make me shudder.

Die Fahne hoch, die Reihen fest geschlossen,
SA marschiert mit ruhig festem Schritt.

[Raise high the flag, keep tight the serried ranks,
storm troopers are marching in calm, firm step.]

How odd that I should remember these words when I have forgotten much that is beautiful and worth remembering.

I also recall a more cheerful song transmitted by what must have been a clandestine sender. It told of prisoners singing the following words to an old German tune:

Es geht alles vorüber, es geht alles vorbei,
Stalingrad im Dezember und Tunis im Mai.

[Everything passes, nothing will stay,
Stalingrad in December and Tunis in May.]

I sang this to myself endlessly. It helped to confirm the allied victories and gave hope that the war must end one day.

Magazines and papers did not often come our way. I still remember one illustrated paper, as magazines were called then, that appeared in the hostel. I have forgotten its title but not its content: at least one article accompanied by a photo. There are certain images that stay imprinted in one's mind that can never be erased, however hard one tries to banish them. I saw this photo six decades ago and it is with me still. Nothing has wiped out the image that was to terrorize me, particularly at night, regarding the fate of those we had left behind. The article described an event in a forest, where Jews had been sent to work. I think it was in the Ukraine. When their work was done, these labourers had to lie face down on pieces of timber tidily arranged in a square. Each then received a bullet in the back of the head and their companions had to lay the next pieces of timber over the bodies and then place themselves there for the murderers' shots that were to follow. This continued until they were all executed. A tall pyre had thus been erected, which was to be set alight.

I think I was 13 years old when I came upon this small piece of a jigsaw, which with thousands of similar pieces was to complete my picture of the Holocaust. I could not disbelieve, and I was afraid for my parents and for all those I knew to be in danger. I destroyed the paper. Not so much to protect my friends but because I felt unable to share this horror, and dreaded any discussion which might make it all the more real.

Most of us had no news from home. Occasionally someone received a Red Cross form with the permitted 25 words, which always said that the sender was well. Such missives could tell us nothing, but at least it was proof, we thought, that someone was still alive. Mina and I managed to keep in occasional contact by that route.

Surprisingly, in the spring of 1941 I again had mail from my parents. Even more surprisingly, the letter was not sent on by some intermediary, it came directly, although it took some weeks, from the distant south-west corner of France, a little town called Gurs, in the Basses Pyrénées. Southern France was in those days known as 'Unoccupied' France, and governed by the French puppet administration set up in Vichy and headed by 84-year-old Marshall Pétain.

In the second autumn of the war, the Nazis conducted an experiment. They planned to make a section of Germany *judenrein* ('cleansed of Jews') for the first time, an experiment with dire consequences. The idea of ethnic cleansing, which more recently appalls us in what was Yugoslavia, is not new. On this occasion the Jewish inhabitants of Baden, the Pfalz (Palatinate) and the Saarland, that is the extreme southwest corner of Germany, were to be expelled from the country. The extermination camps in Poland did not yet exist, and in any case France was closer at hand for this attempt at people-disposal.

On 22 October 1940, the victims in Mannheim had two hours notice, in Karlsruhe only one hour. They were told to pack speedily, only one piece of luggage per person, with clothes, a blanket, food for several days, a cup, a plate and personal cutlery. They were granted permission to take 100 Reichsmarks per person. Everything else had to be left behind. They were not informed where or why they were going.

My mother must have had the anxiety of seeing not only to her own children, Michael and Feo, but also to the orphans who were still in the home she ran. All remaining property was to be confiscated. Everyone had to go: the old, the invalid, the sick in hospitals and the mentally deranged. Almost 7000 were summoned together, the highest number (2000) coming from Mannheim, the city to which so many, like the Oppenheimers, had fled from country districts for the sake of anonymity. That evening the *Gauleiter* (the chief district officer), Robert Wagner, proudly sent the *Führer* a message that Baden was now *judenrein*.

The unhappy, fearful Jewish population was gathered together at different assembly points. In Mannheim they had to meet in front of the eighteenth-century castle, one of the city's treasured monuments, that had once belonged to the elector-princes, the University of Mannheim today. They were eventually loaded onto five trains. Their journey through Germany and France was to take three days and two nights. Some of the sick had been carried to the trains on stretchers. A few SS officers accompanied them. The officers went through the trains, brandishing revolvers and demanding valuables. The law court in Mannheim recorded calmly that on the morning of 22 October, eight Jews had committed suicide by gas poisoning or an overdose of sleeping pills. Others were to kill themselves on the journey.

There are some letters extant in the German Quaker archives about this deportation. They describe the events factually, and include the reactions of local inhabitants. Some said, 'Sie können einem ja leid tun' ('You have to be sorry for them'). Others mocked with jokes about the biblical exodus from Egypt of the Children of Israel. There was no obvious jubilation, rather indifference. Hitler learnt from this experiment that it would be possible to deport all Jews eventually, to any destination, without opposition from German citizens.

Le Camp de Gurs had been set up in 1939 for some of the many refugees that flooded from Franco's Spain across the Pyrenees into France at the time of the Spanish Civil War. The camp was to be a temporary establishment for the summer months. Its official name was 'Centre d'Hébergement', a comforting name: 'héberger' in French is 'to shelter, give refuge'.

The outbreak of World War II a few months later changed everything. The camp was used for the Basques who had fled from their northern Spanish territory, for the *miliciens* who had fought on the Republican, that is the defeated side, in Spain, and for the internationals who had been part of a voluntary brigade, also fighting against Franco.

In May 1940, when German troops overran the northern half of France, those Jews who had fled Germany, Austria and Poland earlier were once more in flight. They made their way south, only to find hostility and internment in Gurs. Vichy was carrying out German orders. It proceeded to imprison those who had fled the Germans, calling them 'les ressortis israélites' ('Israelite nationals'), a nonsensical term created by French officials subservient to the Germans. These *ressortis* were all European. All were hunted. There was not yet such a country as Israel; the Israelites were an ancient biblical tribe. Why were they not honest enough to call them Jews? The bureaucrats eventually simplified this new embarrassing term to 'les indésirables'.

The camp had originally held 4000 refugees from Spain. After the defeat of France, over 12,000 fugitives were now forced into the same place, mainly Jewish women and children. Conditions were primitive, with inadequate wooden huts and insufficient toilet facilities located at a considerable distance from the barracks. Eventually many of the new arrivals were allowed to leave, provided they could prove that they had somewhere to live. Then in October 1940 the Jews driven out of south-west Germany arrived. There were now in Gurs almost 13,000 prisoners, for that is what they had become.

The camp was surrounded by barbed wire. Men and women were separated into different barrack blocks; these too were cordoned off with barbed wire. Some of the inmates were eventually dispersed to other camps in the south: Noé, Récébédou, Rivesaltes and le Camp des Milles near Aix-en-Provence. Today there is little in these quiet towns to remind one that concentration camps once existed there. The French, too ashamed of what they allowed to happen in their midst, prefer not to mark these places in any special way. Many French nationals claimed total ignorance after the war. Today few people living in the region seem to have heard of le Camp de Gurs.

The weary deportees from Germany had left the train at last at Oloron station. They were ordered to abandon their luggage there, and saw it in a large heap, soaked by the rain. They were loaded onto lorries and told their belongings would come later. Many of them never saw their few possessions again, though some of the luggage eventually reached Gurs days, even weeks, later. They themselves arrived in the cold barracks, which were immediately grossly overcrowded. They were to sleep on the bare floors as best they could. Straw was eventually provided to lie on. Later still came the luxury of sacks for the straw. Rats and other vermin abounded. The inmates soon learned that if they tried to save a morsel of bread, they would have to suspend it from a wall. Not a welcome move when some other hungry soul might help himself to the precious commodity.

Eight hundred of the new arrivals in Gurs were to die that winter of 1940, which happened to be the harshest winter of the war. These were mainly the elderly, the sick and the very young. They were not killed, as the rest were to be later. They simply could not cope with the harsh conditions, the lack of food and heating that cold winter. If they were ill, there was little or no medication. There were so many people in the camp that all the tracks between the barracks, and especially to the latrines, had turned into deep mud in the wet winter. Of the new arrivals from Germany, more than half were aged over 60. Old people were often quite unable to make their way through the mire. They lost their shoes in the mud and could not retrieve them. Worse, they fractured legs and thighs in this quagmire terrain and could not move. Death was merciful.

Apparently the food allowance for the camp was not increased for the new influx from Germany. Even the German newspaper *Badische Presse* published a report from neutral Swiss Basle early in 1941 describing the lack of food. It did not hesitate to slander the victims as 'Jewish Marxist emigrants', but prophesied that even without the help of an epidemic the inmates would be decimated by 50 per cent in two years, given the mortality rate.

It is interesting to note that the naming of these victims continued to pose problems. What should those in the neighbourhood who knew of the camp's existence call innocent people who had been driven from their homes quite arbitrarily, starved and persecuted, unwanted in their homeland and unwelcome elsewhere. 'Emigrants'? 'Immigrants'? 'Refugees'? 'Prisoners'? The locals were ready to accept the officially used designation, and showing neither sympathy nor pity also called them, 'les indésirables'.

It was not merely through hunger and disease that the camp lost its population. In January 1942 on the outskirts of Berlin the Wannsee Conference was held. It was here that SS Lt General Reinhard Heydrich, with his assistant Adolf Eichmann and leaders of the SS and the government, discussed the 'Final Solution of the Jewish Problem' in detail. But the death factories had already been established at different locations in Poland: Auschwitz, Belzec, Sobibor and Treblinka. Heydrich announced that all European Jews were to be transported there. These centres would solve the Jewish problem for ever. The Wannsee Conference was the final seal.

SS Captain Dannecker, chief of the Gestapo's Jewish Office in France, kept himself well informed. So when in January 1942, following the Wannsee Conference, the plans for the 'Final Solution' were formulated, Dannecker was ready. He was a true follower of his leader, and knew that Heydrich required 865,000 Jews to be sent from France to the concentration camps of the east. Most of the Jewish inmates of Gurs were to die in Auschwitz. Dutiful Dannecker came to the camp himself, and even accompanied the first convoy all the way. The French government of Vichy had willingly enforced antisemitic decrees, but displayed a token of chauvinist reluctance for the deportation of French Jews, though many of these eventually found their way to death also. They joined those who had been rounded up at German bidding by French police in the occupied section of France. Vichy had no hesitation where the inmates of Gurs, Rivesaltes, Récébédou and the other camps were concerned. After all, they were merely foreigners, not *des compatriotes français*.

From Gurs it was possible to send letters to Britain, as officially Vichy was not at war. The return address started with 'Centre d'Hébergement'. The inmates must have quickly noticed the irony. But we in England, receiving the letters, still had a slight ray of hope, as the word sounded like the comforting German term 'Herberge', also a shelter or an inn. Not that we were completely taken in, as even without any knowledge of French one could understand the word 'baraque', another part of the address.

Not that my parents' letters from France ever mentioned politics. They probably knew what the Germans intended and very likely had little confidence in Vichy France. They did not write what they thought of this because they still wanted to protect us, their children, in the outside world, and because all letters were censored. Not only would the letters not have reached us, the repercussions might have been fatal.

18 Gurs, Rivesaltes and le Camp des Milles

I n their letters, sent under the utmost difficulties, my parents never mentioned the dreadful conditions in which they lived, nor the hunger and privations they had to endure. The letters were usually written jointly to Hannah and myself, also to Aunt Liese in York and sometimes to Mother's cousin Lotte in London. It was only years later that I discovered from survivors, whom I met or through reading their accounts, how impossible life was in these camps. Never did my parents mention their hunger, the cold or the constant threat of disease. Nor that they had to share a tiny space with too many others for sleeping and washing in insanitary, primitive areas. They did not mention the filth, the stench, the lice and the rats. Nor the deaths that took place, 30 a day in that first winter of 1940. Paper for writing was hard to find, so was the quiet space one must have longed for. Fingers were sore and frozen, and the wherewithal for stamps, even when these were available, must have posed problems. The camp was swept by harsh winds from the Pyrenees. There was barbed wire and acres of mud. The latrines at the edge of the camp were inadequate, and for many too distant. The grossly overcrowded barracks were inevitably filthy, not least through the mud. The rain penetrated the flimsy huts. None of this was mentioned.

Instead, they always told us if they had news from Ernest in the USA or Werner in Argentina. Mina tried to keep in touch with them. Giving me Mina's new address in Düsseldorf, Mother asked me specially to write to this faithful woman on a 25-word Red Cross form, the only possible means of communication with Germany. Mother added, 'Mina longs for you all'.

They wrote of my schoolfriends who were with them in Gurs, and mentioned some children we knew who had managed to emigrate to America. They spoke of relatives who had been deported and who were to die. Not that this was said explicitly. The information was, 'So and so has also gone'. Not that we understood the significance of these words.

The notorious conditions at le Camp de Gurs attracted various help organizations. One of the chief among these was the American Friends Service Committee (Quakers), headed by a Dane, Helga Holbeck. They tried to bring essential nourishment into the camp, and were especially concerned for the health of the children. The very young and the very old were dying quickly. So concerned were they that Holbeck and her co-worker and friend Alice Resch, a Norwegian, attempted to remove a group of 50 children from the camp to hide them in a safe place. It was a difficult undertaking and needed much negotiation, even bartering. Not only that: the parents of the children had to be persuaded to part with them. Their last link to a happier past, their only hope for some future life. It must have taken great strength to let them go, to give them up in the knowledge that they might never meet again. It must have needed courage to persuade the children to leave with positive hope and faith in a future. Alice had laid plans for 50 children. At the last moment one set of parents could not bear the parting, and kept their child. They would die together. The children left the camp on a lorry under tarpaulins. It is likely that the camp commandant closed his eyes as they left. They were only kids. Fewer mouths to feed. Who cared?

Alice did in fact rescue 49 children from the camp, my brother Michael among them. She stowed them away into an orphanage called the Maison des Pupilles at Aspet in the Haute Garonne. Alice worked unsparingly for the welfare of these children, as many of them gratefully remember today. The Maison des Pupilles agreed to take the former German, now stateless, Jewish children on condition that the Quakers provided food for all the children, the original French inmates and the newcomers. Alice saw to that, transporting sacks of beans and lentils and anything else she could obtain. She worked tirelessly and apparently without fear, her transport usually a bicycle. Even today, elderly and far away in Copenhagen, she calls the children she rescued 'my' children, and remembers them. I have been thrilled and privileged to meet her.

After half a year in Gurs, in the spring of 1941, my parents were sent to Rivesaltes, another camp, not far from the Mediterranean, in the Pyrénées Orientales. Conditions were also cruel at Rivesaltes, and squalor extreme. In the Mediterranean heat and near the salty swamps (*rives saltes*) there were swarms of mosquitoes and other insects which invaded the many barracks. There was barbed wire everywhere. At that time there were 3000 children in the Rivesaltes camp. Sixty babies died in a few months.

My younger sister Feo was left with my parents, but eventually, when a new opportunity of rescue arose, they let her go too. She was taken from the camp and looked after by an organization called Oeuvre de Secours aux Enfants (OSE, a Jewish resistance group). They brought her further north, to the Creuse region, still in Unoccupied France, and she lived there with other displaced children in semi-hiding. This meant she was alone, separated from our brother Michael, with whom she had shared the horrors of the camp. She was seven years old. My parents were eventually separated, Father into the le Camp des Milles near Aix-en-Provence, Mother to Marseilles.

Le Camp des Milles was an abandoned, dilapidated brick factory. The men slept on the bare floors. Mother was relatively fortunate. She had to live in a designated hostel in Marseilles, but she had a certain amount of freedom. She was able to write to us, and to do domestic work for a young family enabling her to earn a little. Neither parent complained about the conditions. Father wrote that Feo, in spite of her tender age and lack of schooling, sent them the sweetest letters. He cannot help himself, saying, 'I so regretted letting her go from us, the last one of you'.

Mother replied to my remark that I could not imagine being 13 on my next birthday in March 1942:

> Oh my dear child, my experience is similar. I still remember exactly what I was like at 13, because that was the time the family moved to Frankfurt. I thought of myself as quite grown up and was actually very tall. It is nearly three years since we have seen each

other and I am sure you have changed considerably. Through these hard times you have no doubt become a person of greater under-standing, but I am sure you have remained my dear and good child. I am happy to know that you have a good friend. That is something to value. I have true friends and am very glad of them. Even in Rivesaltes I made friends with some very splendid people.

In a letter directed more to my aunt than to Hannah and myself, Mother does let herself go a little with a small complaint:

For me too domestic work is not entirely pure joy, especially when my boss is half my age and considers herself twice as efficient (so much so that I sometimes believe in my own inefficiency. After the past year and a half one can hardly wonder.) I was, however, entrusted with the children, the home and all that went with it when the lady went into hospital. In spite of everything, today's conditions signify a vast improvement for me and I am glad and happy and hope this will continue for a while. It is so irritating that I am separated from Moritz. Hardly anything has changed for him and we see each other only seldom.

She clearly knew how horrific le Camp des Milles was.

It is rare that Mother allows herself an expression of regret, but in this letter addressed to adults (my Aunt Liese and friend), she said, 'Who knows when we shall ever be together with one or two of the children again? Michael is only a relatively short distance from here but we have not seen him in 14 months.'

Again, a later regret: she had received my aunt's good wishes for her fiftieth birthday in May 1942, and replied,

Thank you for your good wishes. I see little chance that they will be fulfilled. But things turn out differently from what we think. Perhaps there will be an unexpected improvement? I would surely never have imagined that at 50 I would be washing nappies in Marseilles for other people's children under laurels in bloom. It is, however, a useful and honourable occupation. In earlier days I have never consciously seen laurels blooming.

In a lighter tone she says, 'I am not displeased with my increasing botanical knowledge, though I would gladly do without the closer acquaintance of some sections of the insect world'.

My father too could joke, though one wonders how. Hearing that his sister-in-law (Aunt Liese) promised to write her memoirs some day, he begged her to be allowed to have the first signed copy, leather bound of course.

Mother was ill in Marseilles. Women did not specify gynaecological details in the past, but I assume she required a hysterectomy rather urgently and was fortunate enough to be relatively 'liberated' (her word) and to be taken into a hospital. She had nothing but praise for her treatment in this French hospital, and was very touched by the kind people who made an effort to see and help her. She praised in particular an elderly cousin of hers from Mannheim, Helene Friedmann. Helene had difficulty walking, but climbed the many steps that led to the ward, insisting on giving Mother the essentials that she herself needed: 'Woe unto me if I protested. Then she treated me as if I were still 11 in our home on the Luisenring! [Road in Mannheim]'.

In the same letter, Mother wrote,

> Just to praise someone else: our Michael is a splendid boy. He sent me a little parcel with goodies that he must have saved literally from his own meals. So I cannot and will not become excited about his lack of inclination to study.

A few weeks later she wrote about my brother: 'Michael seems to be working better at school now, but most importantly he is developing into a person with a good character and a good heart'.

Being a year younger, Michael had had worse problems at school than I. He had missed out on early education because he was Jewish, later because he was German, and then because he was a prisoner.

Feo on the other hand had never learnt to write German at all, but delighted my parents with the thoughts and sentiments she expressed with totally unorthodox spelling and grammar. Despite her youth and immaturity she instinctively knew how to cheer and give a spark of hope to our parents.

19 Oakburn School

We were slowly accepted in Windermere. We had discovered the public library. I remember well that the librarian had looked at us with suspicion when we first appeared. As foreign children who did not 'belong', unaccompanied by adults, we represented a potential nuisance. The librarian felt she had to watch us carefully, but eventually she actually smiled at us and gradually a friendship developed. From being 'foreigners' or 'Germans', we became individuals with names. Together with the humane acceptance we found at our Windermere school, the library extended our world. The books allowed us to escape reality at times, and educated and enlightened us beyond the confines of our narrow hostel world.

Our cultural world included the cinemas. This was one of the few liberal gestures on the part of the matrons. As a cinema owner in Vienna, Mrs Sieber had learnt to appreciate the value of good films. Provided we had saved our few pennies, we were not prevented from outings to see a variety of films. Given my uneasy relationship with the matrons, especially Mrs Urbach, I was often punished by being denied such treats. I was not too upset by this, as Elfi, a good and non-protesting girl who sensibly avoided the punishment that so often came my way, was willing to tell me the story of any film she had seen.

We had our beds next to each other, and she would whisper all the plots to me. To keep the noise down, we often slipped into the same bed, an action that was strictly prohibited. We never understood why this was such a serious offence. Mrs Urbach once discovered two of the younger children in the same bed. This provoked a torrent of scolding. All I managed to gather was that two together in bed was *unmoralisch* ('immoral'). At the time I did not know what the word meant in either language, and the older girls, whom I asked for the meaning, were unable to explain. Somehow Elfi and I continued this defiance; perhaps we learned to be careful. I did want to know what the films that she had seen were about. Unfortunately I often fell asleep in the middle of a scenario, which did not please my friend.

To us girls, school, with its steady routine and its reliable and caring teachers, provided a relief from the increasingly mounting tensions in the hostel. As the war years stretched out, it was inevitable that our unspoken anxieties should grow. There was less and less communication from our families. We thought this was because of the difficulty of receiving post, especially after the USA had also declared war against Germany. We had no inkling of other reasons why letters from parents, brothers and sisters increasingly became a rarity.

At school the English children accepted us. Windermere had become used to us as well as to the many evacuees from the bombarded cities, who vastly increased the population. We still were rather obviously different because of our faulty English, our continental clothes and our names. In those far-off days school registers had mainly British names. One of us, however, had become the proud owner of a genuine Anglo-Saxon name. When Lisl's father, Viennese Mr Scherzer, joined the Pioneer Corps and looked like a true British soldier (well, almost) he became Mr Shearer. This was intended to fool the Germans, should their long-planned invasion succeed or if in combat he became a prisoner.

Lisl, as her father's daughter, also became Shearer. We, her friends, were somewhat peeved, for unlike us she was now doubly blessed. Not only did she own a father, she sported an English name too. We perceived about her a certain air which riled us, as bearers of very obvious German names. Moreover, there was at the time a glamorous film star called Norma Shearer. Where was justice? We released our envy through mockery, calling her 'Norma' in unkind tones. There was some reassurance in knowing that preceded by that very un-English 'Lisl', even Shearer sounded only fractionally more acceptable to English ears than Sophie Goldschmidt, Elfi Reinert and Ruth Oppenheimer, as our foreign names rolled off the register.

We had no close friends among the English girls. This was not due to hostility on their part. Perhaps we were inclined to group together for our own comfort. The others may have harboured some unspoken suspicions about the foreigners. There was, however, one girl who went out of her way to befriend us, Margaret Atkinson. She was shy but very kind. She persuaded her mother to invite the four girls from her age group, Lisl, Sophie, Elfi and myself, to tea. Margaret had a good-hearted, thoughtful and loving mother. Food was not in plentiful supply. All essentials had by then been rationed, but the Atkinsons of Thornbarrow Road welcomed us warmly and showed us what a splendid institution English tea could be. We relished not only the thinly sliced bread and butter, the scones and the cake, the special china tea set that was produced on a pretty lacy tablecloth, but also the warm friendliness we found there. We were well fed in the hostel, but had had little acquaintance with traditional English fare.

Later on, local dignitaries in splendid houses, the Francis Scotts and the Wrigleys also invited us to Christmas parties. The Scotts owned a huge modern farm, well equipped with the latest machinery and tuberculin-tested herds, so different from the farms I knew in the Odenwald or the poorer hill farms that abounded in the Lake District, dependent on the sheep that wandered over the hills. We had never seen an agricultural establishment of such grandeur. We did not know that a farm interior could be so luxurious. The rooms were vast, with elegant rugs scattered over natural wood floors; there were large windows with wide views of beautiful Lakeland country. The actual farm buildings – we were allowed to see the animals – seemed so clean and hygienic, there was no pervasive cattle smell.

The Wrigleys had acquired wealth through industrial effort in Lancashire, the next county south, and their Victorian neo-Gothic house with its high pointed windows startled and impressed us. It was the type of house one could marvel at from afar, through the bars of great iron gates or from hilltops. A vast, grey stone pile with turrets and dormer windows, and beautiful old trees around, lending charm and protection, the whole a setting for an imaginary fairy tale. We felt overawed by the grandeur as we walked up the long gravelled drive and entered through an arched, ecclesiastical doorway, and into a polished hall that was large enough to take a school assembly. None of us had ever seen a complete suit of armour holding a spear, though I was relieved to notice that the apparent mediaeval knight on guard duty was empty. In spite of war and restricted labour, a maidservant brought in the party treats that we were to enjoy, and the family themselves organized children's games. No word was ever spoken about our background, nor were questions asked about ourselves. There was genuine kindness, but we were treated as specimens rather than individuals. This was partly due to a lack of understanding of who we were, but we had all also been in the country long enough to recognize, even as children, the depths of English reserve. We were quite happy to be generously entertained and fed as a social group that deserved a charitable outing.

In the 1940s and for some years after, the official British school-leaving age was 14. Hostel girls reaching this level of adulthood had to give up the security of school. Some of us simply stayed in the house to do the necessary domestic chores. Others found work in the village, their tiny wages contributing to our living expenses. We had had our minimal but well-intentioned education of the three Rs.

When it was my turn to leave school, Miss Webster, our kind head-mistress, told the hostel matrons that she would like to try and transfer me to a secondary grammar school. She felt I had the ability to cope with the academic demands and that this would be in my interest. The matrons agreed. They always enjoyed praise for the hostel, even if it came for one of their least favourite charges. Local children attending the grammar school went either to the nearest, Kelsick School in Ambleside at the head of Lake Windermere, or the High School in Kendal, an eight-mile train journey to the south.

Miss Webster took me to both, and both rejected me. In Kendal two imposing ladies looked at me hard and tut-tutted because I had never learnt a foreign language. English did not count, and the fact that I did have a non-English mother tongue also counted for nothing. I had not touched the science subjects, and my mathematics consisted of arith-metic only. I was almost 14 and an academic grammar school started for pupils at age 11. My inability to speak and write English had helped me fail the required examination three years earlier. The real problem was that even in extenuating circumstances one could not make an exception for a German child. They did not need to add that after all this was the enemy. I was disheartened, but Miss Webster remained undaunted and determined.

Next on her list was a private school: Oakburn, in Windermere. This school was very small. Two principals, Winifred Brett and Elizabeth Knox, ran the school. They did this with energy and goodwill and a rather nonconformist ethos. Miss Knox was a Scot from Glasgow, Miss Brett was from Newcastle-on-Tyne. There were boarders and day pupils. Some pupils were there because of the constant bombing of their home towns. There were wartime regulations, transport difficulties and food rationing. Teachers for small private schools were not easy to come by: many of them were required to do war work. Because Miss Brett and Miss Knox took a great personal interest, there were few examination failures. The girls would say they dared not fail. Children who had been unhappy elsewhere or had not done their best seemed to manage at Oakburn. It was expected of them. The school was also the least ex-pensive in the Lake District. I think the principals were ignorant of the current rate of school fees, and were too busy teaching and organizing.

Miss Brett and Miss Knox, their names conveniently abbreviated to the collective 'Brox' by the pupils, looked at me hard. They understood only too well that I had missed out on education, that in some areas there would be years of work to be made up. They knew that if I came to the school I would have to work hard and so would they. It was all some-what daunting. Even worse, they thought Miss Webster was asking them to take me without fees. She was not. Optimistic Miss Webster assumed the money would be found, though I had no idea from where. Brox explained that they had already taken on a refugee child, Hannelore Kamke, originally from Danzig (today Gdansk), who had come to them through the Save the Children scheme, a charity they had long supported. Hannelore had fled first from Germany to Denmark with the other pupils of the Walkemühle Schule, a small but progressive school whose pacifist and internationalist ideals were anathema to all the Nazis stood for. When the Germans occupied Denmark, the school had been forced to flee again, this time to Wales, where the teachers, as German nationals, were immediately interned as enemy aliens and the pupils scattered. Hannelore was not a Jewish child. Her mother had had the courage to be openly anti-Nazi, and was persecuted. She escaped to France but was eventually caught by the Germans. Her father did not share his wife's opinions and lost touch with his daughter. Brox had taken in others at reduced fees, as they were children of friends and relatives in the northeast and Scotland who had suffered from air raids. Miss Knox eventually looked at me and said, 'Will you worrrk?' Not really knowing what she meant and hardly understanding her Glaswegian accent, I replied that I would work. They said they would accept me if someone were prepared to pay my fees.

In spite of all the burdens Miss Webster had to bear in a difficult job under wartime restrictions, she was willing to champion my cause. She approached the hostel matrons to ask whether there was anyone connected with me who could provide the necessary money. My aunt could not – she hardly earned the sum of even those low school fees which were ten guineas a term (a guinea was one pound and one shilling). The matrons wrote to the Jacobson sisters in London, who had not only helped me, but also a number of others, to leave Germany. Only one of the two sisters was working, but they discussed the matter with friends. Mrs Margaret Buck of St Albans, a relative of theirs by marriage, offered to guarantee my school fees for the next two-and-a-half years. It seemed the most amazing good luck, and was indeed the best thing that happened to me in England. Mrs Buck's generous offer even bought a bicycle for me to cover the five-and-a-half-mile ride to school.

Oakburn was to provide the key to my future. My life there was very much happier than anywhere else in England up to then. I enjoyed the challenge of new subjects. I took to French far more readily than I had taken to English. Mathematics and literature gave me real pleasure. Science remained a secret to me, as to my companions. The school did not have the financial resources for even the pretence of a laboratory. Brox taught us almost everything themselves, including daily games of hockey in the winter and tennis in the summer. Sometimes we were spared by the weather. It is the wettest region in England.

A puritanical atmosphere pervaded the school. We were not excused from activities we did not like. A major event of the school year was a full theatrical production. Conscious of my still imperfect English, and given my general unhappiness, which was evident in my appearance, I hated to appear on the stage. I thought it reasonable, when so many of the girls were stage-struck, that I could be excused. Not at all. Apparently it was good for my character to do what I did not enjoy. (Character building was a great feature of the school.) The first part I was allotted was a cannibal in an A. A. Milne play. For this I did not have to speak English, I had to growl and yell in cannibal language 'Boriah, boriah boo!' (Some of my contemporaries thought it a suitable part for me. Wasn't I 'foreign'?) I thought these stupid words had been specially designed to pinpoint my inadequacy and increase my misery. Even worse, I had to dance in a jerky, wild manner, arms and legs akimbo, alone on the stage, exulting over the missionary I was about to consume. Much as I adore the music of Schubert, I still shudder when I hear his ballet music to *Rosamunde*, the cannibal dance accompaniment. My supreme effort on the day of the performance was not to burst into tears on stage.

Worse was the next annual play, *The Merchant of Venice*. I hated the play then, and although I have seen it several times I still have an aversion to it, in spite of some excellent actors who attempted to interpret Shylock as a grossly persecuted victim. To me it expresses antisemitism of an early kind. Who can blame Shakespeare? He had not met any Jews. They had been banned from Britain long before, and such knowledge as there was had been effectively taught by an anti-Jewish Church. It was felt that I could hardly complain about the role I was given, the Prince of Morocco, one of the unsuitable suitors for the heroine Portia's hand. Again a foreigner. Rehearsal time was agony for me, as the teacher tried publicly and not without ridicule to improve my foreign accent. I had to stand amidst gaping pupils practising the sound 'r' in a less Germanic and guttural fashion. Nor was it easy to watch as the girl playing Shylock was told to adopt cringing or fawning 'Jewish' attitudes. Because the *Merchant* has an uncomplicated story line, it is popular in British schools, a less difficult Shakespeare play than most. I have seen it taught in other British schools, and I know that antisemitism is part of it, often by well-intentioned but ignorant teachers.

Nor did I want to go swimming. In the summer we were sent daily into Lake Windermere (rain offered no respite from this routine). I had hoped my experience of near drowning in that lake, and its extreme cold, might provide sufficient grounds to escape this torture. I should have known better. It was cold indeed at times. We swam by the calendar and not the temperature. I am sure there was occasional snow on the mountains at the far end of the lake in May, and we knew that the water from up there could only come one way. Nevertheless, I did learn to swim, and was grateful for that.

In those dreary war days, the school felt it right to have a compulsory course in dancing. This was a special type of dance, based on movements portrayed on ancient Greek vases, known therefore as 'Greek dancing'. It was meant to allow us free rhythmic expression, a happy escape into a world of fanciful beauty. For this exercise, we were scantily clad in a garment known as a 'chiton', an ancient-Greek-type tunic. As far as I remember, our pale green silk – or in wartime artificial material – chitons were fixed on one shoulder, sleeveless, revealing much adolescent flesh, as they barely reached our thighs. Free expression consisted of leaping as butterflies, prancing as gazelles and swaying as delicate daffodils. Taller than most, I had absolutely no wish to express myself as a bumblebee or any other treasure of natural life, and remained graceless, grumbling and glaring. Our teacher, Miss Stanley, was a joy to watch, and I hated disappointing her. I had one success in several years of struggle with and against Greek dance, as a good, solid oak in a storm, moving my arms only. My legs stayed firmly rooted as the tree's foundations.

But my time at school was essentially a happy time. The atmosphere was so relaxed. The girls laughed so often. I was not used to that. In the hostel laughter had become rare. Even in actual lessons there seemed to be time for jokes and fun. What is more, our classes were calm, with no sign of excessive discipline. In such an ambience it was easy to learn and behave well. The teachers, especially Miss Knox, were willing to discuss with us, to hear our questions and be prepared to accept our challenges. I was not used to adults who treated children as equals. It was a stimulating and exciting new academic experience. I relished what I learnt, I enjoyed the work and began to see what this new world might open for me in the future, in spite of lack of family, in spite of war and danger.

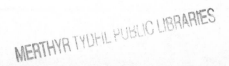

As schoolgirls, we were at ease with one another. This was a special relief from our wary behaviour in the hostel. In school we were carefree, in the hostel restrained. Even as taboo a subject as menstruation could be easily mentioned – although every girl called it the 'curse'. At the age of 16, we had the facts of life explained to us, admittedly remotely and very seriously. We were brought singly into the private sitting-room of the principals and given a leaflet with tiny print and diagrams – no one wasted paper in wartime – produced by a national education authority. For this solemn occasion there was no opportunity for questions or discussion. I understood very little, but felt I had been initiated into the adult world. My further education eventually came from continued reading of all manner of literature.

There were lessons that Brox did not teach themselves. Specialists were brought in for music, art, tennis coaching and riding. The money provided for me did not stretch to such extras. I longed for piano lessons, but they were beyond my reach. Yet poverty has compensations: I was deeply grateful that I did not have the wherewithal for riding. Never a trace of envy did I feel as I saw the jodhpured girls, armed with riding crops and confidence, proudly mount their horses and bounce away – only relief.

Uniforms were standard and obligatory. With the help of the school, I had various cast-offs. As the name 'Oakburn' implied, it had to be brown, and I wore the gloomy dark colour like everyone else. I actually liked it, for all the wrong reasons.

Best of all, I found my first real friends outside the hostel, friendships that have stood the test of time and are mine still, even with those who made homes in the most distant parts of the globe.

I cycled to school with Ruth and Winifred Lowe, who were actually neighbours of the hostel but whom we had not previously known. At Bowness, the next village, Evelyn Waters always waited for me beside her bicycle. She and her sister were in Windermere as evacuees. They lived with an aunt while their parents stayed at work in Southend on the Thames estuary, where bombs were often jettisoned just before the German planes returned to their home territory. There was another day girl (Oakburn was mainly a boarding school), Pat McEvoy, who became a friend and has remained so, even in distant Australia.

I was grateful to these new friends. They invited me to their homes and were good to me. I do not think that they were informed about my background, though they understood that I was far from my family. They were too tactful to ask questions that might have caused pain, and I simply could not tell them of my well-grounded fears. The subject was and remained taboo. But above all, I enjoyed my new studies. Literature, French, mathematics and Latin were exciting, and extended my limited world. I may not have cared for the stage, Greek dancing and swimming, but relished the physical challenge of tennis and hockey. Brox and Oakburn School helped to transform my life then, and promised a better future.

20 The final truth

I soon realized how very privileged I was to be enjoying my education beyond the age of 14, when I should really have left school. I knew this was not fair to the others, who had ceased their education at that point, especially Elfi, my closest companion in age. Elfi knew it too, and for a while my happy schooling created a rift between us. In the evenings I spent long hours on homework. Not only did Oakburn School have high expectations of us, I had years of work to make up. My genuine delight in my scholastic work and the time spent on it inevitably created a distance between my contemporaries and me. Unfortunately the matrons too felt they had been unwise to allow me to continue such privileged schooling when everyone else had to leave and earn a living. To make this vaguely fair, I had to do quite heavy chores morning and evening, which I accepted totally. Every morning it was my job to clear out and re-light the boiler that supplied the hot water. I also looked after the Esse cooker that was never meant to go out and had to be cleaned carefully in the mornings and fed with anthracite. All other fireplaces that were used in the house were cleaned and reset by me. (Central heating in older houses was rare in Britain.) From the cellar, I daily carried a hod of coke for the boiler, anthracite for the cooker and coal and wood for any remaining fireplaces. I joined the others in vegetable cleaning and dishwashing. All this was a price for attending Oakburn School that I was more than happy to pay.

I relished my cycling to and from school. Some of my cares dissolved away from the hostel. One could hardly have had more beautiful surroundings. As far as Bowness, I rode along Lake Windermere, England's longest, with glimpses of the Cumberland mountains. I learnt their shapes and their names, and looked on them as individual friends. They looked different every day, blue and distant, or almost tangibly close. Sometimes of course they simply were not there – mist or rain had swallowed them and an opaque cloud lay on the water. From Bowness to the school there was a considerable climb. It was challenging to see how long I could keep cycling before gradient and exhaustion forced me to jump off my bicycle. In spring there were wild daffodils on the roadside, blossom on the trees. Rhododendrons everywhere. Near the school I enjoyed the thrill of cycling through an avenue of laburnum, which I called my tunnel of golden rain (in German laburnum has the prettier name of 'Goldregen').

Returning from school was usually less happy. The feeling of dread returned, increasing as I cycled back more slowly. I feared daily that I would be in trouble with the matrons, that I would be found wanting in some way. All too often my foreboding proved accurate. It was my turn to be a focus for trouble and blame. Life became increasingly difficult and unhappy. I was not always able to do my homework adequately. 'A big girl like you should not be at school any more.' And I was constantly scolded just for being there. My status was neither wanted nor accepted. The school, on the other hand, continued to show remarkable understanding.

Towards the end of the war, I had a wonderful surprise, a totally unexpected experience. A visit from my eldest brother Ernest. Ernest had joined the US Army and had been shipped to Europe once the 'second front' had been opened in Normandy. On his first 'furlough' – a new American word to add to our ever-increasing vocabulary – Ernest came to England. It seemed too wonderful. He had all the right attributes for wartime Britain: he was male and American. The matrons too appreciated these qualities, and were pleasant to him and therefore not unpleasant towards me. It was quite impossible to tell him what conditions were like for me. There were more important things, after all, war and fighting, war and separation, war and death. He arrived in Windermere with Hannah, having visited her first in the south of England. It seemed incredible to me to have three siblings together. It was strange suddenly to acquire a feeling of respectability, which the presence of an American military uniform seemed to bestow, quite different from being a German child on one's own, a nobody. The visit certainly compensated for some of the wretchedness I had been feeling. I started to believe again that there might be a chance of being reunited with the whole family when the evil war was over. The end was beginning to be in sight. I was longing to write to my parents about our meeting. But for some time now we had not been able to be in touch with each other.

By the second half of 1944, more joy. We heard that our younger brother and sister, Michael and Féo, were alive and safe. Féo, now officially and openly in France, had to add an acute accent to her name. France had been gradually liberated. A French family, the Sommers, had promised my mother, whom they had met in Marseilles, that if anything happened to my parents they would look after the youngest children if, as French Jews, they themselves did not perish. There was no news from my parents yet, but these were strange times. Confusion and chaos reigned. Parts of France were liberated, parts were still held by the Germans or their collaborators. The Sommers were fortunate: they survived and kept their promise. They knew where Michael and Féo were. When Paris was finally free, Robert and Paulette Sommer took the two children with their own large family back to the capital.

Brother Ernest visited them there on a later furlough. He arrived at the door, which was opened by Féo. It was a home that entertained many passing strangers in those strange days. Ernest thought the child was his sister, though the six-year separation had caused him doubts, but was somewhat stunned when she suddenly disappeared and left him standing. Féo had gone to tell the others, 'I think my big brother has arrived'. She was ten years old and had last seen him more than half a lifetime before, when she was four.

From our parents, still no news. I was the first girl in the hostel to trace her siblings in continental Europe, and did not then appreciate my remarkable good fortune. Lore, Daša, Annie and Margot each had a brother in England whom they rarely, if ever, saw. The others, some of whom had left siblings behind on the continent, were never to see them again. My brother and sister, Michael and Féo, had been found. This gave us hope that others might also have survived.

Now, in April 1945, news was coming through of the liberation of the concentration camps and the horrors witnessed, particularly at Bergen-Belsen, as it was British troops that arrived there first. The shocked liberators could barely take in what they saw. They filmed the place in all its horror, its mountains of corpses and its few ragged skin-and-bone survivors, their bodies and faces hollow, their eyes huge. These films quickly appeared as newsreels in British cinemas, Windermere included. The matrons insisted that we were all to attend such a showing.

My mind and emotions rebelled. I resented this order bitterly. We had some idea of what had gone on in the camps; we certainly knew the significance of the names Buchenwald and Dachau. We had heard of thousands dying of disease and degradation, brutal atrocities and starvation. But I complied. We all emerged numb and silent from the cinema, and remained in that state. For the matrons who had sent us to see the films, I felt anger. Today I am not sure that they were wrong. Hopefully, I looked to them for words of comfort, but they had none. How could they? They were as deeply affected as we were. Numbed, we were unable to discuss even with our closest friends what we had seen and read.

But one day, not long before the end of the war, a telegram arrived at the hostel from the Swedish Red Cross. They had taken Lisl's mother from Auschwitz to Sweden. She was very sick, but she was alive. We had no notion what Auschwitz meant, but here was the best news anyone had ever had. A living parent had risen from the hell that was Hitler's Europe.

Lisl was not in when the news arrived. She was working as help to a Windermere dressmaker. Because I was the owner of the only bicycle, I was told to fetch her. I remember only crying and laughing when I dumped my bike and ran into the startled dressmaker's workshop. I hugged Lisl before I could utter a word. Through my tears I told her the news, with the growing realization that my mother too might be found. Lisl froze, went pale, and gradually her tears began to trickle down her expressionless, unbelieving face.

Back at the hostel it was like a carnival. Lisl was still speechless, though now smiling broadly. But behind the outpouring of joy there was an unspoken thought shared by many of us: to have had one parent preserved and living, accessible in England, was good fortune, to find a second, on the continent of war-torn, death-infested Europe, was a miracle. Could divine justice not have been spread a little more evenly? It was difficult for us children, who had heard nothing from any parent, not to think so.

The war in Europe ended on 8 May 1945. People celebrated wildly. At long last the destruction, fighting, killing and murder had ceased. The hostel girls were happy of course that the war was over at last, but foreboding and fear overshadowed our joy. What were we going to discover? How long were we going to continue living in the hostel? Where would we go when and if we found surviving relatives? What would happen if we did not? We had become accustomed to not formulating these questions aloud.

On 11 August 1942, our mother had written her last letter from Marseilles, from anywhere, I imagine. She had sent it to cousin Lotte in London. It was meant not only for her, but also for Mother's sister Liese in York and her friend Mrs Schwarzwald, for Hannah and myself, and generally for all the Oppenheimer children.

> Dear Lotte,
> It is days now since I have wanted to reply to your dear letter, and for unimportant reasons I have not achieved it. Now everything has been overtaken by new events and I am turning to you all, to you, to Liese, the children and Mrs Schwarzwald. It is only by coincidence that the envelope to you Lotte is already franked. I am thinking of you all with intense love. Once again we are facing a new turning point in our destiny and we have to move [*Wandern*]. It may be that the children [Michael and Feo] can stay where they are, and I may perhaps be able to decide for myself. I shall try to remain with Moritz. The children shall continue to preserve contact, as they have done till now. I do not have to tell you, Ernst and Werner, to keep a special place for them in your hearts. They shall be good human beings – and in spite of everything – shall become good Jews and think of us in love, as we shall be thinking of them.
>
> Feo's address is now Chateau du Masgellier, par le Grand Bourg, Creuse, Unoccupied France.
>
> Michael: Maison des Pupilles, Aspet, Haute Garonne, Unoccupied France.

I kiss you in love and tenderheartedness and shall love you ever more, the more distant and harder our separation.

Your mother, sister, cousin and friend

Grete

I think at the time I could not or would not see the real import of her letter. It should have been obvious what had happened. I did not realize, at the age of 13, that this letter was written before a deportation.

Not long after the end of the war, I heard from Monsieur Sommer in Paris, that as a lawyer he had tried to find out what the fate of our parents had been. From the French Police Headquarters he learnt that my parents were taken from le Camp des Milles (where my mother had voluntarily joined my father) on 12 August 1942, although their train did not leave till the thirteenth for Drancy, the notorious assembly point outside Paris for all deportations. M. Sommer wrote, 'De Drancy ils ont été déportés par les autorités allemandes pour une destination inconnue, le 17 août 1942' ('They were deported from Drancy by the German authorities for un unknown destination, 17 August 1942'). I am sure the information from the Police was correct. They had after all been closely involved.

For years we did not know what this 'unknown destination' was. But the Germans had filled in their lists efficiently. That is how I learnt that my parents left France with convoy no 20 from Drancy for Auschwitz on 17 August, with 1000 Jews. A good round number. In the cattle wagon they spent two days in a closed, dark and crowded space, without food, without water in a very hot August. More than half the group happened to be children, 207 boys under 16 (of which 154 were less than ten years old). The age groupings are specified, the youngest three boys being two years old. There were 323 girls under 16. Here again the ages descend to two. The list is classified by nationalities: the majority were German, from le Camp des Milles. I think Mother did not have to go then but wanted to be with Father, whatever his fate. Many of the children were without their parents. One truck contained 46 children and one woman. It was the Vichy government that had willingly delivered the Jews from its territory to the executioners.

As always, order had to be maintained, and the Gestapo had detailed lists of all those on a deportation train. Family and first names, dates of

birth, country of origin and nationality were stated. As these nationalities and names of towns as well as other spellings are in French, one
must assume that the Germans who supervised the deportations had
help from French minions for this clerical work.

These lists have survived unexpectedly. Copies accompanied the
train, and were eventually destroyed after the arrival and death of the
prisoners at the extermination camp, usually Auschwitz. By chance the
original lists remained in Paris and were found long after the war and
compiled into a massive book (80,000 victims), entitled *Le Mémorial
de la Déportation des Juifs de France*, collated and published (in 1978)
by Serge and Beate Klarsfeld. Serge, now a prominent lawyer, had a
special interest, his father being one of the deported. In these lists we
found the names of our parents, and there we learnt what their fate
was. Convoy no 20 arrived at Auschwitz with my parents on 19 August
1942. At least 900 people, including all the children, were immediately
gassed. By 1945 there were three named survivors, names I do not
recognize.

Still known as VE Day, Victory in Europe Day, 8 May 1945, should
have been my mother's fifty-third birthday. She was not to reach it. Her
fiftieth was her last. We kept hoping for a long time. It was not till many
years later, on seeing *Le Mémorial* that I knew exactly what my parents
had to face. I am glad I know.

Accepting these deaths was difficult for all the hostel girls. We could
never be totally sure. There was no official statement, no positive proof.
Soon – but for most of us unwilling to accept the hard facts – we had to
understand that all our parents had died, as had siblings, grandparents
and members of the wider family. They had been killed most brutally, had
starved or been worked to death. The news on radio or in the papers was
loaded with horror. Our imagination did not have the capacity to deal with
it. It was all available but impossible to accept, to believe at a personal level.
Deep inside me I knew it was true, but spent years hoping and making up
impossible stories of how my parents were perhaps lost somewhere, were
ill and could not explain who they were, were unable to speak, or had
forgotten where they once belonged. By some coincidence or miracle,
we would find them one day. It was a vague and transient comfort, as
daydreams are.

We did not talk about this bereavement amongst ourselves. We had after all always feared that this would happen. We remembered the death of Sophie's mother, in her forties, a death probably not unconnected with her suffering. Sophie now had to accept that she had also lost her father and her only brother, Manfred. The girls who had already had a parent living in England, and Lisl, who had found her mother, a survivor of Auschwitz, had departed. The rest of us knew that our fears had been justified. The pain was very present. To this day I have not discussed this loss with my friends. I imagine they too did not talk about it with their nearest and dearest. We have all told our children where we came from and what had happened to us, but we have not expressed our pain or our grief. The dread of reliving the pain was too great.

Because I lost my close family brutally and inexplicably, I always felt that funerals are an unnecessary indulgence. I now realize how wrong I was. A funeral offers a finality that may enable one to look at a future beyond. It is a form of acceptance of death. We experienced bereavement without end. There was no funeral and no mourning, instead grieving in secret over what had to stay concealed. The death was always there. Unmentionable. No one broached the subject with me. Not in the hostel, where we were all in the same situation, not at school, where I was the odd outsider, not later. Some of the good friends I was to make as a student must have realized what had happened, but questions were not asked, the subject was not discussed. I am sure the intentions were honourable and well-meaning. Eventually I stayed in the homes of friends, whose families by their kindness made me feel that sympathy was there. The family into which I married seemed to find my background embarrassing to deal with. It was not a topic for discussion. When I met members of my own family again, my siblings, we obviously had the same hesitations and inhibitions. We were unable to communicate our grief. We did mention our parents, but always in as objective a manner as possible. I could not speak about this death, even when I wanted to, as I knew that I would break down, I would be overwhelmed by the loss. It was there, a huge barrier to be skirted.

I remember well the first social occasion on which I was able to mention the fate of my parents naturally. I had been invited to a party with people I did not know. The conversation turned to aged parents and their problems, a conversation in which I rarely take an active part, but someone asked me about mine. I had no choice. 'They perished in Auschwitz when I was a child,' I replied. The questioner was stunned, but actually interested, concerned. My hostess turned the conversation and made it clear that my words were in bad taste.

Writing a lifetime later, I am beginning to understand that few, if any, could cope with this history. It was not to be a topic in Germany for many years. In the countries where many victims had sought refuge, they found that no one wanted to hear their suffering. Those who had survived miraculously against all the odds felt they could not impose their memories on the fortunate who had not experienced the horror.

I did not myself live through the worst horrors that the Holocaust had to offer. I did, however, have more experience of grief and pain, of loss and deprivation, of humiliation, despair and abandonment, than any child should ever have to face. Some of these feelings have remained, and after writing of my experiences I am slowly beginning to understand why I still cannot speak of my parents or of their fate without losing control. If I had been able to unburden myself at the time, to express my grief, to mourn, to question openly the obscene inhumanity, I might today be able to speak rationally of the past, to integrate it into the sufferings of the many other victims that I have known, or whose stories I have read. I doubt I would ever have forgotten the past, but I would perhaps have become more objective, less traumatized.

21 End of war, end of childhood

I n March 1945, not long before the war ended, I reached my sixteenth birthday. By then it was clear that Germany was more or less
defeated, but I still had to register as an enemy alien, and was
obliged to report weekly to the Windermere police. There I had to
produce my new aliens' registration book, with my gloomy photograph
attached, in which the police duly entered the date of my weekly appoint-
ment with them. The process was taken seriously and handled with
bureaucratic earnestness. I had been riding my bicycle to school for two
years, and now I needed permission to do so. Geography was one of the
precious new studies I was able to follow at Oakburn School, and from
my sixteenth birthday, as an enemy, I required special dispensation to
possess an atlas.

The war was over in Europe in May. The following August, after the
cataclysm of the atom bomb, fighting ceased in the Pacific. The time had
come to look forward. Girls gradually left the hostel, either because they
were old enough to be independent or had found relatives in the USA,
Australia or New Zealand. Not one of us left in the hostel at the end of
the war, except Lisl, found a parent or any other relative alive in Europe.
The three Roth sisters had departed earlier, and we heard years later that
their father had been among a handful of survivors of a concentration
camp in Poland, sick in body and spirit. He had lost his wife, his eldest

son and the two youngest of his original family of six. The Adamecz sisters also lost their youngest sibling, Gretel, who died with her mother. At school, the other German refugee, Hannelore Kamke, learnt that her mother had died in Ravensbrück, the notorious concentration camp for women near Berlin.

If my sixteenth birthday brought new anxieties, my seventeenth was worse. I was still at school, and therefore not contributing financially to the hostel household. I realized this, but was helpless – I had been allowed to pursue my education. But in spite of that, I was a constant object of harassment. A few days before my birthday I received an ultimatum from the matrons of the hostel. It was quite simple: 'You either leave school on your birthday, or you leave this house'. I do not know whether the Newcastle committee responsible for us had been consulted, though I am sure Mrs Urbach and Mrs Sieber could have made a good case. Of course I had no choice. If I remained at school, I would have nowhere to live. And although semi-adult, I was penniless.

I informed Brox, the principals, that I would have to give up my schooling. They were indignant. In that case, they said, I could live with them. This generous offer overwhelmed me. It was evident that this was a sacrifice. Not only was I an extra body to feed and to house, I was bound to intrude on their privacy. In any case, they already had one refugee girl in their home, and I did not think Hannelore Kamke would appreciate me as an interloper. On my seventeenth birthday I left the hostel. Before leaving I was summoned into the presence of both matrons. To make their case slightly more democratic, they had called in the eldest of the girls, Margot Hirsch, to be a witness to my disgrace. They told me in dismissive language that I was to leave the hostel that had sheltered me, that I was ungrateful and did not appreciate the good home they had given me. They did not find an actual crime to pin on me, but there were variations on my ingratitude. Both Mrs Sieber and Mrs Urbach expounded on the same theme, and looked to Margot for approbation. But Margot said nothing. Nor did she defend me. We had been together for seven long years, there had been bonding and intimacy, but the indoctrination that authority was always right had a strong hold. We had been trained to be obedient, and when in doubt most of the girls took the side demanded and expected. To be safe. The other girls were discouraged from saying goodbye to me. I felt betrayed, especially by my closest friends, but they were frightened, though at the time, in my hurt, I thought them cowardly. They dared not risk disobedience. We were powerless children still.

I was unnerved to be facing a new life. But for the first time I was to experience an unaccustomed sense of freedom, and saw opportunities ahead that I had not thought possible earlier. This new-found freedom, however, was to have its twists and turns.

Mrs Urbach and Mrs Sieber were unable to reconcile themselves to my leaving the hostel with such evident relief and enthusiasm. This was obviously the behaviour of an ingrate. It could not be tolerated. A letter consequently arrived at Oakburn School from them. It said that a Jewish child ought to celebrate the coming festival of Passover in Jewish surroundings, and that I was to come back to the hostel for the requisite eight days. This time I knew the English word hypocrisy, and recognized its significance. Jewish religious observance was not a major feature of hostel life, and I sensed instinctively that this was not the genuine reason for my call to return. It was sinister. I refused to go. Miss Knox pointed out, reasonably, that she had to comply with the request. She was not my legal guardian. I was still in the charge of the Newcastle committee, with whose approval the letter had been written. Very reluctantly I agreed to return.

A scolding reproach would not have surprised me, nor a sermon on ingratitude. What I did not expect was the bizarre punishment meted out, though it was in keeping with the prevalent nineteenth-century ideas on bringing up difficult children. I was put under *Zimmerarrest* ('room arrest'), locked up alone in a room for a week. Of religious practice, not a whisper. My new-found protectors had assumed I was back to celebrate the festival of Passover, happy with my old friends. The matrons were angrier than I had expected. The few girls still living in the hostel were not allowed to communicate with me. They were afraid even to try. Again I felt betrayed. These were my friends, my almost sisters. Elfi, who had been my best friend, occasionally brought a tray with my meal. I could not believe that she would not speak to me, that the injunction to exclude me had to be obeyed. Was this more important than our friendship? She was no longer a child. Was it resentment because I had left and tasted freedom? I understood that she envied my opportunity to be educated, for which I do not blame her. We had all adapted in different ways. Some of us accepted fatalistically the uncertain existence that we led. Many worked hard, immersing themselves in various duties, hoping to escape censure. Some learnt the art of flattery and survived. I understood that this worked, but I had enough of the sullen teenager in me to make me incapable of uttering what I considered untruths. My priggish fulminations against insincerity did not impress those of my companions who had found a way of coping.

Vienna was famous for its easygoing life and work style, but Mrs Urbach and Mrs Sieber had become harsher as the years went by, and less tolerant. They had looked after us for many years, over seven altogether by the time the hostel was dissolved. They had been tied to this job because it fulfilled the conditions of their domestic permit. They had no special knowledge of raising children. For their own sons they had had the benefit of domestic help. They were not experienced with girls, and certainly not with emotionally challenged youngsters. Nor could they feel rewarded as one after the other the girls left, without regret, without sentiment, more likely with relief. Increasingly I was aware of the difference between the upbringing of children in England and continental Europe. Had the matrons accepted some of the harsh teutonic, not to say fascistic, discipline prevailing over there? Order and total obedience, as in the Germany we knew, seemed all-important to them. We had occasional fun in our early years there; there had been childish play and pleasure, but as the war years dragged by we became sadder, and some of us quite withdrawn. The bitter war news, the years of responsibility in a hard task, a task they would never have chosen voluntarily, the distance from their own family and friends, took a toll of Mrs Urbach and Mrs Sieber too. The latter often remained in her room, not well, apparently. Here she was, landed with domestic chores for children she could not possibly love. How she, the *grande dame élégante*, missed the adulation from the visitors to her cinemas as she presided in style over various foyers. She had often described her glittering Viennese evenings, as she demonstrated little dance steps to us and swirled around the bare kitchen of the home, eyelids low in remembered rapture. We were captivated, with our noses pressed against the screen of her memories. We, her willing audience, such wretched substitutes for past admirers.

And somewhere deep inside us, sharing her sadness, we the children stayed quiet and considerate. She sighed frequently and dramatically, and some of us reacted with true or false sympathy. She was not above a theatrical pose: once after some child's transgression, clutching her brow, she declared, 'So people unburden themselves by sending their children to us. And what of us? We are supposed to transform them into paragons. What expectations!'

The ladies did believe in the potential of the sow's ear, but we in turn showed little inclination to be turned into silk purses. Mrs Urbach looked after Mrs Sieber, willingly and with more solicitude and affection than she ever showed any of us. We noticed that she longed for some affection herself, preferably from Mrs Sieber, and was sad when it was apparently not there. To me personally they seemed cruel. Their harsh abuse of power came straight from the harrowing fairy tales of the brothers Grimm. And I found my own helplessness echoed in the experiences of the young victims in those stories.

My incarceration lasted a week. Meals were left outside the door, but I was not hungry. I had had the forethought to bring my schoolwork with me, expecting to fit it in occasionally. I did not know that I would have such a long stretch to study. For the first time in my life I made a conscious effort to learn long poems by heart. My selection happened to be the French Romantic poets. On the whole they were mournful and suited my mood. There was Alfred de Vigny's 'La Mort du Loup' ('Death of the Wolf'):

> Hélas! ai-je pensé, malgré ce grand nom d'Hommes,
> Que j'ai honte de nous, débiles que nous sommes!
> Comment on doit quitter la vie et tous ces maux,
> C'est vous qui le savez, sublimes animaux!'

> [Alas, I thought, in spite of the great name of Man
> That we bear, I am ashamed of us, for we are weaklings.
> How we should leave life and all its ills,
> You, sublime creatures, can teach us.]

Then I memorized 'L'Expiation' ('Atonement') by Victor Hugo. Where de Vigny was sad and bitter, Hugo was tragically lugubrious, with his long, drawn, plaintive vowels:

Waterloo, Waterloo, Waterloo morne plaine!
Comme une onde qui bout dans une urne trop pleine,
Dans ton cirque de bois, de coteaux de vallons,
La pâle mort mêlait les sombres bataillons.

[Waterloo, Waterloo, Waterloo, dismal field!
Like a vessel filled and boiling over,
Encircled by woods, hills and valleys,
Pale death came indiscriminately among the dark battalions.]

No doubt it was good to learn that not everyone thought of Waterloo as a splendid victory.

I was grateful to leave the hostel a second and final time after I had served my 'sentence'. The hurt I felt at what I thought then was a betrayal by my friends meant that I lost touch with most of the remaining girls, in spite of the fact that seven years together at close quarters had almost made us a family unit. But this state of hurt did not last, and eventually I made contact again with those who had been my closer friends after we were scattered through the country and the world. The hostel was finally dissolved a few months after I left. Mrs Sieber moved to London and Mrs Urbach to California.

Some years later I heard that Mrs Sieber wanted to see me, so I visited – we both happened to live in London. Neither of us mentioned hostel life, for good reasons. I did not want to be in touch with Mrs Urbach, and in any case there was little opportunity. I once tried to do something for Mrs Urbach. Not long after I left the hostel, I found her cookery book in Bumpus, a once well-known Oxford Street bookshop. The book was published after the war, but still not under her own name. I remonstrated with the manager that the book should not be sold under a false name. How could the unsuspecting man have known this? Obviously he was totally unaware. It was clear that he thought I was an eccentric or worse. Bookshops do attract oddities. When I found the book again, some years later, I took action and wrote to the Austrian publisher, complaining. Of course I had no reply.

With the war over, the hostel terminated, childhood, such as it was, ceased for most of us. It had not been a golden period, and if we were to know moments of nostalgia they were very selective. Yes, our lives had been spared. Were we grateful for this? It is difficult to be sure. I think there was a constant sense of guilt that we had survived when our parents had not. In my rational moments I knew that I was indeed fortunate. My brothers and sisters had escaped the Holocaust, but they seemed so far away.

Brother Ernest was a good man. Our parents had disappeared. At the time we had no details of their fate, so Ernest felt responsible for the family of siblings. He tried to gather us together in spite of the fact that he had a hard time making a living for himself, his wife and baby daughter in New York City after he was discharged from the army. His family was increased by the arrival of his parents-in-law, who by a miracle and through an exchange of prisoners had survived the concentration camp of Theresienstadt. They were old, sick in mind and body, and did not speak English. He exerted himself for them, but still endeavoured to obtain visas for our entry to the USA; and he succeeded, in part. Werner was delighted to join his older brother in North America, after almost ten years of solitude and separation. He had struggled so hard to prepare a farming life for us all in Argentina. He had worked tirelessly, without social distractions and in primitive circumstances. He was bitterly disappointed that his efforts had not helped our parents to leave Germany. He gave up all that he had worked for and achieved, to start afresh in the USA in the proximity of some members of the family. Hannah had also worked seriously at farming jobs in England, having to earn her living from an early age without completing the education that would have been hers had times been normal. She took up Ernest's invitation and emigrated to the USA in 1947.

Michael (now Michel in a French context) and Féo in Paris had the same opportunity of another *Auswanderung*. In their young lives they had suffered more than the rest of us. They had had longer experience of the Nazis, a period in the camps and time in hiding, avoiding the deportations. They had frequently hungered, and had to face the trauma of separation early in life. They knew hostility from the Germans and the French. They had lost their family and their language. But they found a new family, and French had become their means of communication. Should they risk losing this second family? Should they forsake yet another language? It seemed too much to ask, and Michel and Féo stayed in France. They are now French citizens.

Ernest, Werner and Hannah became Americans. Britain may not have been too keen to accept refugees in 1939, but in 1947 the British government once again showed its humanity. Parliament passed an act, quite unobtrusively, permitting those children who had come to England with the *Kindertransport* and who had lost their parents to become British citizens without having to endure the usual formalities of advertising publicly, official interviews and much expense, an unparalleled humane gesture. And thus I became the only member of my family to be a British citizen.

In the intervening years, we have all seen each other again. These were inevitably sad as well as joyous encounters. However, we have never met again as a complete sibling group. There has not been a total family reunion. Those of us who have survived are always happy to be in touch. We have had very different experiences, different education and upbringing, different cultures, and we all interpret Judaism in a variety of ways, yet we are surprisingly alike. Although we have lived apart so long, our thought patterns are similar. We often say the same things at the same time. We enjoy the same jokes. Our political views are related. Féo and I seem to have the same dress sense, though my friends say I have none.

We had to acquire three new languages: Spanish, English and French, but we no longer have a common language; German – our mother tongue – has been put behind us, and we do not communicate as easily as siblings should.

We have been strewn around by the winds, made new homes, created new families. That is the pattern of human evolution. We would have preferred a different route.

Epilogue 1:
survivors in the
Diaspora

After the turbulence of the war, we tried to adapt to our new lives. We were grateful to have survived, though few of us could believe that we had been specially favoured or had deserved survival, when we knew that our parents, grandparents and siblings had perished. I knew what had happened to my own parents and where Aunt Ida and Uncle Gustav eventually lost their lives. Helene Friedmann, the very elderly and dear relative of Mother's, who had survived Gurs and had taken care of Mother in hospital, was also deported and presumably died. All remaining relatives who had not been able to leave Germany perished.

My family, in spite of brother Ernest's efforts, was never to be re-united. It was to be a long time before we could make any attempt to meet more regularly. Our first priority was to survive the survival, to make new lives for ourselves. Travel overseas to see our siblings was a luxury for later in life. We had all managed to see one another again, but we had not been able to meet as a whole clutch of siblings, a real family group, as Werner and Ernest unfortunately did not grow old. Ernest died of a heart attack before he reached 60. He had been in the American army and had taken part in one of its last and worst battles in Europe, the Battle of the Bulge in the Ardennes. Originally, as the eldest son, he had been training to take over our father's factory. Having had this future stolen, he emigrated unqualified to the USA. His life there had not been easy before he joined the army, once the USA was forced into the war. After being discharged, he struggled for the rest of his life. He had to work hard to look after his family, which now had five members with the survival of his wife's parents. In spite of all his effort, the American dream passed him by.

Werner, having spent years on his own in Argentina, much of it in toil outdoors, did not find it easy to adapt to life in urban America. He too struggled to live the American dream, managing to fight off tuberculosis. But as an industrial worker he fell victim to mesothelioma, an asbestos-related disease, and died at 62. Both brothers struggled in circumstances that neither had willingly chosen.

Hannah took her chance to emigrate to the USA, and also arrived there without qualifications. Her schooling had ceased long before it should have done in Germany. Her work experience in Britain of hard agricultural labour was not appropriate for life in New York City. She attended evening classes, worked as a nanny, as a cook and on a sewing machine in a sweat-shop factory. By studying at night, she was able to take up sociology at Cornell University and work her way through her college years by looking after a family with five children. She qualified as a social worker, dealing with those on the margins of society. Now retired, she still finds time to do voluntary work for the elderly. For her at least, America provided a kind of comfort.

Michel and Féo stayed with the Sommer family in Paris. Michel, who had missed more schooling than his brothers and sisters, had a tough time in the rigid French education system after the war. Deprived of many years of education and everything else that belongs to a normal childhood, he had to sit in a class with children years younger than himself, to make up for what he had missed through war and incarceration, though he was a lifetime older in experience. Understandably, he hated the process. He became a glass-blower, showed great talent, and went on to make all manner of scientific apparatus and instruments from glass, many to the individual requirements of research scientists. In time he founded his own successful firm, and is now a father and grandfather.

Féo married very young. The Sommers introduced her to a rabbinical student with whom she has created a good and loving home. She is much in demand by her children, her daughters- and sons-in-law and grandchildren. In addition, elderly ladies in Paris in need of help seem to look in Féo's direction and she appears.

As for me: a US visa arrived at the same time as a scholarship to Bedford College, University of London. I chose to study, feeling this was an opportunity not to be missed, but fully intending to emigrate to the USA after I had graduated. But I did not leave. Somehow, my life had been forged in England, the country had been good to me, I had acquitted myself reasonably well, teachers were in short supply. So I launched myself into the teaching of modern languages. It felt right to do this, to let my skills help repay the debt I owed to Britain.

My Aunt Liese Krämer in York was able to give up domestic work. Schools as well as individuals clamoured for teachers of German after the war. She had more offers to teach German than she could accept, and her life was transformed. In spite of all that she had suffered at the hands of Germans, she had a deep love and understanding of German language, literature and music. She taught enthusiastically, and happily rode to work and everywhere else on her bicycle, till she died at 70. In a way, she had never left Germany. Its culture and civilization had provided her with an anchor in exile.

My cousin Lotte Oppenheim in London, on the other hand, continued to clean and cook for families with grand names in the capital. The end of the war saw her very alone; her employers knew and cared little about her. Before the war she had been unable to bring her elderly father to safety, as she had hoped. He and the rest of the family were deported; history did not tell Lotte where her family was killed. She was 91 when she died, and bitterly unhappy.

Not a single member of my family had been in a position to make plans for his or her future. We would surely not have chosen to leave our homeland, to disperse in all directions away from those we loved. It was circumstances in the form of Nazi persecution that orchestrated our lives and deaths.

And what of the hostel girls? Most of us did not know where or how our parents died. We faced endless feverish flights of imagination. Conjecture turned into nightmares. Inevitably, we also followed patterns set for us over the centuries by our ancestors, as they were persecuted, cast out and killed. We scattered, as they had done before us.

The three Roth sisters found their father. He was broken in body and spirit in a concentration camp in Poland from which few had survived. He had lost his wife, an older son and two infants. His daughters did not know him any more. They lived together in London, where the three girls all married very young, as if desperate to start afresh as quickly as possible. Friedchen died before old age. Lea married a young Auschwitz survivor who had come through the camps protecting his blinded younger brother. Lea's husband was not going to abandon this boy now. So from the start, the marriage included the handicapped brother-in-law. Hilde, the eldest, who from the age of seven had never let her younger sisters out of her sight, was able at last to leave them and move north with her husband and have a home of her own.

Only Lisl was to retrieve her mother. She joined her father as soon as he was released from the Pioneer Corps. When at last Britain allowed her mother to enter the country – the tuberculosis she had caught in Auschwitz had prevented her from entry – they decided to move to Palestine/Israel, where they coped. Their attention and interest as a family was dedicated to making Mother's life as normal and bearable as possible.

For the rest of us it took time to adjust to this parentless future. The majority of us stayed in England, with Sophie the only one faithful to the north. She became a nurse, married and lived in Barrow-in-Furness. She did once visit her former home in Langensellbold (Germany), where doors and windows were alarmingly shut against her, and someone called out 'It's all paid for'. She had not even asked. At 70-plus, she still bears me a slight grudge for preventing her escape to London as a 14-year-old when she was deeply unhappy in the hostel! We had little choice as to where to go. If we had relatives anywhere in the world, who actually wanted us to join them, we did so. If not, we made our way to the larger cities, where we might find more companionship or work opportunity than in post-war Windermere. In any case, few of us had known happiness there.

Elfi, when the hostel closed, moved into lodgings in London, worked in an office and then became a primary schoolteacher. Like the rest of us, she blended from extraordinary formative years into a life of ordinary routines.

The Adamecz sisters were still children. When the hostel finally closed they found no relatives to look after them, and were moved to yet another institution in Manchester. For a while Ruth was taken on as a domestic servant, but was eventually offered a scholarship to the local art school. She soon had to give up because her hostel neither allowed her the time nor the opportunity to do the college work expected. Eventually both girls emigrated to Israel for life on a kibbutz. They both married there. Ruth stayed in the kibbutz, as far as possible from Windermere and the matrons. Her bitter memories of the Windermere hostel remained with her. Both girls had been unhappy there. Ruth had been bitterly wretched as a child, responsible for her little sister during all those childhood years, never able to say to her mother, as she had yearned to do once war had ended, 'I did look after Inge as you wished. She is happy and well.' Their mother and sister had been murdered. They never knew what happened to their father, who as an 'Aryan' had abandoned them. They themselves had found a route to survival, but it was hard.

Eva Less, who had nursed in London, found Canada welcoming to nurses. The other two girls from Berlin, almost identical in age and friends, Marion Mendelssohn and Paula Katz, also went far afield, Paula to Australia (Sydney) and Marion first to Africa, then to Australia (Perth). Neither knew of the other's existence in the same country. Both died young.

Annie Heufeld, my favourite among the older girls, who sewed for us and kept a protective eye on our activities, emigrated to the USA after falling in love with a GI who was a professional musician and a refugee from Vienna. Her husband, Rudi Fellner, became a music professor, in Louisiana and later Pittsburgh, Pennsylvania. Annie continued to sew, but now it was costumes galore for operatic performances. She has retained the wide smile and the warmth that had comforted some of us as children.

Lore Freitag left the hostel to join her aunt and uncle in New Zealand. She was 13 years old, and did not see her parents again, in spite of the promise they had given her, which had helped her to survive the anguish of separation. She was to become one of New Zealand's most distinguished speech therapists, but she also died too young.

Dasha (she had abandoned the Czech spelling) lived on her own in London, and also trained to teach, before meeting a student whose family had originally fled from Berlin to South Africa. She married him and started a new life in Johannesburg. But this *Auswanderung* was not final. They eventually moved to a freer and happier world in Australia.

Most of us have met again, so we were able to learn about our intervening lives, our views and our beliefs. None of us has forgotten her history. Nor do we cease to be grateful for rescue and survival. We may differ in our political, national or international views. We are deeply conscious of our Jewish history and the injustice of persecution. We view our own personal Judaism in varied ways. Some of us are orthodox, some more modern in our views, some agnostic. We bear a history that we cannot forget or deny, though some of us are less open about it than others.

The story of these women, my hostel friends, like that of my own family, is the perfect example of the Jewish Diaspora. It is the reply to the oft posed question, 'Why are the Jews to be found everywhere?' We had not intended to move to the far corners of the globe. We had no choice.

Epilogue 2: Germany

Some former refugees after the war felt incapable of ever facing Germany or Austria again. Others thought, as I did, it was not only possible but also important to return – a very individual sentiment. Our erstwhile homes were never far from our thoughts. I fully understand those who do not wish to set foot in Germany. For years I felt the same.

My first return was accomplished with the help of my earliest English friends, Margaret, whom I had met on my first day at Bedford College, and Alan Forrest, her fiancé and later husband. They lived and worked in Germany in the fifties. They invited me, with considerable persuasion, to visit their home in Cologne. I was not coming to a part of Germany that had ever been a part of my life. Thoughtfully, they proposed that I travel to Brussels, where they would collect me, thus avoiding any opportunity for me to encounter German officialdom on my own at a border or an airport.

Driving over the Belgian border into Germany made me feel tense, even afraid. I recognized the houses, the tall gables with attic windows in the steep roofs. As a child, once I realized I was not wanted by the inhabitants of my village, I thought that these narrow, steep gables with their two small windows as eyes, were tight, frowning faces that looked down at me and disapproved. The older houses looked gaunt, just as I remembered them. It was 18 years since I had left the country. I no longer felt the disapproval, but I recognized the severe faces. They still frowned. The fields were so neatly delineated, no rambling hedges or tottering dry-stone walls that I knew so well from the north of England. The kitchen gardens were so very tidy, the vegetables neatly arranged, almost regimented. Seeing shops with the proprietors' German names made me feel ill at ease. Our name had not been allowed to continue. It had been expunged. More than once I wondered why I had come.

A few days into my trip came the highlight of my stay. I was to meet Mina again after the endless years of separation. The Forrests knew what Mina had meant to me, and had looked for her and found her. She was in fact the only German I had wanted to see. I suspect she was also the only one who wanted to see me again. She had last seen me as a child, and now I was a woman of 28. She was working in the kitchen of a hotel in Niederbreisig, a pretty tourist destination on the Rhine. We had arranged to meet Mina after work. But when we reached the hotel, the proprietor shook his head. Not yet. Mina had not finished washing up. It was against the rules.

When she did emerge, enveloped in a large apron, just as she used to wear for her domestic work in our family, she was an old woman whose face bore set lines of hard labour and suffering. She was smaller, heavier, and the light rapid step had disappeared. We barely recognized each other, but flew together, embraced, hugged tightly and sobbed. We had met in the hotel foyer, a public place, and seemed rooted to the spot. The Forrests quietly melted away to explore the little town. Mina took me to her little attic bedroom, where there was solitude and stillness. It was difficult to speak, we were barely capable. The questions we wanted to ask each other were too painful, and we had to make do with tears for the years of separation, the suffering and the loss. It was not easy to begin talking, we both started, then we both hesitated. We were overwhelmed by sorrow and regret. There was the unspeakable gap of 18 years during which both our lives had altered beyond our worst imagination. I should have liked to ask her so much, but her answers, even had she been able to give any, would not have lessened the pain. The pain was not mine alone, and I fear I did little to alleviate hers.

In her room, Mina looked through her pitifully few possessions and came up with an unexpected treasure she had guarded faithfully for 17 years. It was a large office-type hard-cover ring file, and inside it lived my family. Like many who had been forced to separate, those who remained kept and cherished their letters. My parents had preserved all the letters that the first emigrant, Werner, sent from Argentina, then Ernest's from the USA, later mine, in a very childish hand from Tynemouth and Windermere, and finally Hannah's from the south of England. They had also filed carbon copies of letters they had written to the older boys, asking them for advice on how to escape from Germany, and begging them to do their utmost to help the family to find refuge. On 22 October 1940, the day of deportation, when my family had to leave their last German abode, Mina appeared. How did she know? How did she dare? To be *judenfreundlich* ('friendly to Jews') was a crime to be punished with prison or concentration camp. Mother thrust the file into her hands, asking her to look after the precious load. There is a wealth of memory in that correspondence – a résumé of our early exile, a litany of longing and ever-dashed hopes. Very few deportees have had the chance to find such trusty hands to guard their one and only inheritance.

Mina's was a sad life. How she must have missed our family, which had also become her family. Unlike so many Germans, she had paid not the slightest attention to Nazi attitudes towards us. Those few brave Germans who continued to help Jews, or who risked death by hiding them, are not generally recognized as heroes in Germany even today. As a Roman Catholic she stayed true and faithful to her Church, but I doubt if her Church ever recognized Mina for her love of others, the rejected and persecuted, when such devotion was forbidden by the laws of the land.

Mina and I separated – yet again – with difficulty in that little hotel on the Rhine. As we hugged and sobbed again and looked at each other through our tear-filled eyes, we knew that our lives could never be intertwined again as before, however much we would have wanted it. Seventeen dreadful years could not sever the bond, but they did give us both different directions.

We stayed in touch by letter – not easy, as she wrote with difficulty, in pencil using the old gothic script. She wrote in formal, polite terms, unused to natural letter-writing. Questions would have been inappropriate, but letters were a sign of life.

Then a few years later Mina's letters ceased. My own letters went unanswered and there was no word from the proprietor of the hotel where she worked. When I decided that she must have died, it was, for all its sadness, an easy transition. For in reality Mina's death had begun all those years ago when she had been forced to leave us.

My brother Michel had crossed the frontier from France to Germany much earlier. I know his suffering had been greater than mine, but he was more tolerant and far-seeing, and knew that not only did he need to return, the Germans needed us. Some of them even wanted us. He took his young family to Fränkisch-Crumbach quite early on, and met Crumbachers who were friendly and to whom he could relate. He could not remember the village as well as I do, being eight years old when he left. But he had some curious experiences. People seemed to know who he was, the rumour of his arrival had spread immediately. At one point he wanted to make a purchase in the only local shoe shop. He thought of himself as an unknown customer, a foreigner, and an out-sider with deficient German. He was about to state his shoe size, when the shopkeeper said, 'Your father's size was 43'. My brother was stunned. How did the shopkeeper know that this man with French-accented German was my father's son? It was two decades at least since Father had bought his last shoes there. How did he remember? And why?

Twenty years later, in 1978, Michel managed to persuade me to accompany him and his wife on a very brief visit to Fränkisch-Crumbach. I was most apprehensive, but knew he was right. What surprised me was that the village was so unchanged. There were some concessions to the second half of the twentieth century: the roads had been tarred, there were cars and garages that had not existed before, as well as television aerials. Otherwise it looked as it had over 40 years earlier. I knew every street, every corner. It was all familiar, yet all alien.

I could remember names of people but would not have recognized anyone. Yet we were recognized. The news rushed through the village that 'Ruth and Michael' were back. The surname seemed unnecessary. Where else would one remember children who, aged eight and nine, had left a place over 40 years previously? We spent the night in Fränkisch-Crumbach's only hotel, a concession to modern times non-existent in our day. The manager inadvertently called me Frau Oppenheimer, not the name on my passport or my reservation. We walked along the Allee to look at our former home. People appeared, shyly asking, 'Do you not remember me?'

Then Heinrich Hartmann, the son of our one-time immediate neighbours and Hannah's former friend, emerged. He looked as if life had not been easy for him. He had spent his war years on the Russian front. He brought me an old, fingered sepia photograph of the four younger Oppenheimer children taken in front of our house in the Allee. I could not believe my eyes. Did he remember his close ties to Hannah? His sudden rejection? The time when we were not just *personae non gratae*, but invisible? What made Heinrich keep this photo? Did he ever miss us? I could not ask him. I took the picture gratefully, had copies made, then sent the original back to him.

I never heard from him again, nor did I see him in the years to come. Subconsciously we both must have realized that too much had happened in the intervening years for any childhood bond to survive. Perhaps the effort to stay in touch should have come from me. But I could not bring myself to force a friendship with homes from which so many years earlier we had been rejected. When in later years I was doing a reading in the school of Gross-Bieberau, an adjoining little town, a polite young student came up at the end of the lesson and introduced himself by telling me he lived in Fränkisch-Crumbach at Allee 39, knowing I would recognize this as the house next to ours. Surprised, I replied, 'But that is the Hartmanns!' 'Yes,' he said, 'I am the grandson'. So I asked him what he knew about us. Nothing apparently.

People spoke to us hesitantly. The words 'Hitler', 'Nazi', 'persecution', even 'Jews', were not spoken. One could only risk the word 'damals' ('in those days'), with a shrug of the shoulders and an averted glance. In the circumstances, I assume, this was tact, fear and perhaps a little shame.

Our former neighbours across the Allee, the Schnellers, invited us into their home and were friendly and hospitable. I remembered Helmut, now the head of the family, who as a child had played with Michael until this too was no longer permitted. He did not seem to remember that their friendship ceased. Had he forgotten that his father was a strict Nazi? I did not have the courage to remind him. I know that Michael missed Helmut's friendship. Helmut's wife, Antje, herself a refugee from the

Sudetenland at the end of the war, had been ousted by the Czechs as Germany was defeated. She showed sympathy for our plight. I was amazed to discover how much she knew about our family. She had listened to tales in the village, and asked questions. I am sure this stranger to the village knows more about my forebears than I do, though I suspect she heard less about what actually happened to us. I sometimes wonder what tales their children have been told about us, and why on subsequent visits I have heard people say, 'We did not ask you to go. You left of your own accord.'

Clearly some Crumbachers were glad to see us. Others felt it would have been better had we stayed away. Not that this was said to our faces. As we walked down the Allee, we passed a house where the traditional German window shutters were closed. We noticed that there were two sets of fingers clenched through the slats of the shutters. Obviously someone was attached to those fingers and was standing watching us, hidden from view. We walked on. I turned round inquisitively and noticed that the knuckles still showed. Whose were they? And why was it not possible to view us openly, to speak to us perhaps?

Two years later, in the summer of 1984, I returned once more to Fränkisch-Crumbach. This time my stay was to be more prolonged. I had come with my friend Eva Rogers, a journalist, who wanted to accompany me on a visit to places that evoked painful memories, to help me come to terms with the past and to let me talk about it for the first time. She later wrote about our visit ('The Return'), and I was grateful to her. Her writing helped me to face what I thought I had forgotten or suppressed.

We stood outside my original family home, and I described it to Eva. The present owner of Allee 37 happened to see us and talked to us. He does not live there but rents out the property. We were invited to the house nearby where he lives. His wife showed us photos. They had of course no direct link to the past. This was a constant refrain. We were allowed to visit my former home, or at least the upper half; the house is now divided into two apartments. A curious feeling to see my first home again, the place of my earliest memories. I had not wanted to leave it at the time we were forced out, and now these memories came rushing towards me. Again when I told the current tenant, simply by way of explanation, that I had lived there as a child, she vehemently said, 'I do not know anything about that'. Of course not, I reassured her.

Eva had the courage that I lacked. It was she who insisted that we call on the new owner of Father's factory, Gerd Goetschmann, a young artist and craftsman. He had acquired the premises to turn them into well-designed and environmentally friendly living quarters. Some of the glass-roofed rooms, built like that to give the maximum light to the workers who did the finishing of the cigars, were to be turned into studios, the best of all possible solutions for a location that is still known three generations later as the Oppenheimer Fabrik ('factory'). Gerd was a thoughtful man, concerned with confronting the past and the history of his country as well as its future. He was not a native of the village and was considered an outsider; he did indeed hail from 40 miles away, not from the Odenwald. Gerd had wanted to learn the Oppenheimer story from the other villagers, to piece together what had happened to us. 'Don't worry your head about them,' he was told, 'they are all filthy rich in America'.

Gerd had hoped to affix a modest plaque to his premises to commemorate the Oppenheimer connection. He was warned that he would have his windows smashed if he did so. So instead he went one better: he engraved a copy of Picasso's 'Dove of Peace' into the facade of the factory, the bay window of what was once my father's office.

I had returned, in spite of myself and against all my original intentions. These journeys were far from easy. My brother Michel was right: the past as well as the future had to be faced. Trying to ignore my childhood experiences, to suppress horror and hatred, could not be the way forward. My fear, though unreasonable now, had not abated, but I knew it could be overcome with time, encouragement and a beckoning hand. And the hands beckoned in unlikely places and friendship burgeoned. Slowly I visited Germany again, though mainly in districts unfamiliar to me as a child: Cologne, Krefeld, the Saarland. Germans of the post-war generation wanted and needed to meet survivors. They had been told little by their parents and grandparents. Perhaps a sign of shame and remorse. I was asked thoughtful questions and was willing to answer. In England such questions had been rare. I could sense compassion and a desperate realization of what had once taken place in the *Vaterland*.

It had taken me a long time to return to my one-time home, and I had not achieved this entirely through my own volition. But I had seen enough to know that it was a different place, that there were people who wanted to see me, talk to me and know me.

Now that the first steps had been taken, I was beginning to think that it had not been a foolish dream to return, but a very positive experience. I was not sure that I would make the effort again, soon, but need not have worried, as quite unexpectedly I started to be invited. All over Germany there were good people who felt that history could not be ignored. They started to research and enquire, and when the opportunity arose to contact former inhabitants the opportunity was seized.

In 1988 I came to Fränkisch-Crumbach again, this time to commemorate the fiftieth anniversary of Kristallnacht. The *Bürgermeister* gave us a reception in the new Town Hall, my first school. It was a curious feeling for me to walk into a building which I had been forced to leave in disgrace 54 years earlier. My new friend from the village, Hilde Katzenmeier, had come uninvited, to support me. The *Bürgermeister* explained that he was one of those born later, with the implication that what had happened to us was not part of his experience or knowledge. He related the history of the village, with exciting tales of mediaeval robber barons, but history apparently ceased in the sixteenth century. There was no reference to the Jewish community that had once been an integral part of the village, no word about the synagogue or the industry that my family had provided. There was no echo of Hitler or the Nazis, no mention of the many enthusiastic party members of the village. The word 'Jew' was withheld throughout. I felt it would have been in bad taste to raise a question. The *Bürgermeister* was, however, thoughtful enough to have a private word with me, recognizing that I had been a child of the village. He whispered to me that his mother remembered my family. We drank a toast to end the proceedings and guests and hosts alike seemed relieved that it was over.

In the *Heimatmuseum* ('local history museum') there are exhibits of old crafts and trades. The Oppenheimer factory, the first real industry and largest employer of the area, does not rate a mention. This absence must be obvious to the locals. There is a photographic display of all the mayors who have ever held office, among them the enthusiastic local

Nazi Party leader, Herr Trinkaus, who had made Father's life impossible in Fränkisch-Crumbach.

But try as it might, Fränkisch-Crumbach cannot divorce itself from me and my experience.

For many years my German friends had endeavoured to mark in some small way the building that had once been a synagogue. The dwindling Jewish community had to sell it to the local café proprietor in 1936. It was therefore spared from destruction in November 1938. The group devoted to this commemoration project hoped to enable the post-war generations, the majority of the village, to know what the purpose of the building had once been. They had wanted to affix a modest marker. It had not been possible to do this, as the owner, Herr Ripper, like his father the original buyer, had refused permission. The former synagogue was not to be visited or discussed. But the committee persevered with its project, often in the face of non-cooperation and refusals as well as lack of involvement by the local powers, who had to think about their votes. Instead of a plaque on the actual building, they set up a beautiful memorial granite stone opposite. The following words were inscribed:

SHALOM
FRIEDE
DAS HAUS GEGENÜBER DIENTE DER
JÜDISCHEN GEMEINDE FRÄNKISCH CRUMBACH
BIS 1936 ALS SYNAGOGE
ZUM GEDENKEN DEN VERFOLGTEN
UND ERMORDETEN JUDEN
ZUR MAHNUNG FÜR DIE LEBENDEN

SHALOM
PEACE
THE HOUSE OPPOSITE SERVED THE
JEWISH COMMUNITY OF FRÄNKISCH-CRUMBACH
AS A SYNAGOGUE TILL 1936
IN MEMORY OF THE PERSECUTED
AND MURDERED JEWS
A REMINDER TO THE LIVING

There are those in Fränkisch-Crumbach, who want to forget, who say it is time we 'drew a line under the past', or who insist with a new-found nationalism that those who teach or talk about the Nazi past are committing the sin of *Nestbeschmutzerei* ('soiling one's own nest'). But there are the others who know that we must not forget the past, that to do so will encourage a repetition.

The dedication of the memorial in that small town in Germany took place in November 1991, on the fifty-third anniversary of Kristallnacht, and 50 years after the Wannsee Conference at which details of the 'Final Solution of the Jewish Problem' were decided. Survivors had been invited. Though some sympathetic German visitors came from afar, there was still a certain unease about such an event, and by no means everyone turned up from the locality. Not even the *Bürgermeister*, perhaps conscious of the next elections. Traffic had not been diverted – that might have made the proceedings too official. But it was a solemn and moving occasion nonetheless, with a choir and a band and serious speakers. The important lesson that could be drawn from it was stressed by the Protestant minister, Herr Kunz, who quoted from the Talmud: 'Forgetting leads to banishment. Remembering hastens salvation.'

He solemnly pronounced the names of those Jewish inhabitants of the village who had lost their lives in the Nazi concentration camps. He thanked those of us who were linked to the dead for coming, 'Without hatred but with pain and grief in your hearts'.

As with other survivors, the pain and grief live with me still, and always will. I cannot forget what happened to me as a child. The experiences have shaped me, and probably in some respects my own son and daughter too. I realize with gratitude that I would not have them any different. I know too that I have been fortunate. I have experienced goodness and kindness from strangers. I do not claim to be whole, though healing has taken place through them – but above all, and quite unexpectedly, through my friendship with good people from Germany.